Realistic
Business Dictation

Doreen Sharp & Doreen Trimnell

Pitman

PITMAN PUBLISHING LIMITED
128 Long Acre, London WC2E 9AN

A Longman Group Company

© Pitman Publishing Limited 1985

First published in Great Britain 1985

British Library Cataloguing in Publication Data
Sharp, Doreen
    Realistic business dictation (2000)
    1. Shorthand—Pitman—Examinations, questions, etc.
    I. Title   II. Trimnell, Doreen
    653'.4242'076   Z56.2.P5
                 ISBN 0 273 02173 7

Printed and bound in Great Britain at The Bath Press, Avon

INTRODUCTION

Realistic Business Dictation is designed for speed building after the basic shorthand theory has been completed. The material incorporates all the first 1000 words of the *Word Division List of Canadian Business Vocabulary* and almost all the *700 Common Words* (newly published list) together with derivatives.

The material presents a great variety of realistic office work. It is written in a straightforward style and includes letters, memoranda, reports, circulars, notices, leaflets etc. Each of the twenty Units is based on a different type of business.

The passages included in *Realistic Business Dictation* vary considerably in length. A few 'new words' are introduced in each Unit which are not included in either the 1000 or 700 word lists. These words never total more than six for any passage and are treated as 'known' outlines in subsequent Units.

The longhand is marked off in tens to allow for dictation at varying speeds according to students' requirements. The syllabic intensity ranges from 1.27 to 1.57, with the bulk of the work in the 1.3s and 1.4s, counted on the total number of words in each passage. The word count and the syllable count (SI equals Syllabic Intensity) are both given at the end of each piece of work.

It is suggested that students should prepare for dictation by reading and thoroughly practising the outlines for the 'new words' and any other outlines with which they may be unfamiliar. Before dictation is given it is important to drill the new words using the phrases (see Appendix, page 108) and/or sentences from the passage. The work can then be dictated at suitable speeds according to the students' progress. Office style dictation should be introduced as well as regular timing.

Additionally, cassettes are available which provide dictation in a variety of voices. Units 1–10 are dictated at 50 wpm repeated at 70 wpm and Units 11–20 are at 60 wpm repeated at 80 wpm.

Each Unit can be used for typed transcription training and the addresses for all the letters are given in a section at the beginning of the book. The addresses have been carefully chosen for each Unit and cover many parts of the UK. Students are expected to set out the correspondence correctly and paragraph appropriately.

LIST OF OUTLINES (page 79)

This is a combination of the first 1000 *Word Division List of Canadian Business Vocabulary* and the *700 Common Words*. Those outlines from the *700 Common Words* not already appearing in the *Canadian Vocabulary* are shown separately after the main list in each alphabetical section. Words set in italic are from the *700 Common Words*.

The few words that have not been included in the dictation material are marked with an asterisk.

ACKNOWLEDGEMENTS

The Authors would like to offer sincere thanks to their many friends who have granted them the privilege of browsing through their correspondence to ensure that this book contains genuinely REALISTIC BUSINESS DICTATION. Grateful acknowledgement is also made to Mrs M E Witham for her help in transcribing all the passages into Pitman New Era and Pitman 2000 shorthand. Finally the Authors wish to record their gratitude to the Editor, Pam Wickham, for guiding them so smoothly through the work for this book.

ADDRESSES FOR TRANSCRIPTION LETTERS

UNIT 1   ELECTRICITY BOARD

1 Mr W Black, 2 Saleyard Cottages, Pandy, NR ABERGAVENNY, Gwent, NP7 8DR
4 Mrs R Stanton, 16 Station Road, Gilwern, ABERGAVENNY, Gwent, NP7 0HD

UNIT 2   BUILDING SOCIETY

2 Miss Sally Day, 30 Egerton Road, Eastham, SOUTH WIRRAL, L62 0BY
5 Mr James Strong, 4 Sefton Way, Thornton, LIVERPOOL, L23 4TJ

UNIT 3   GARDEN CENTRE

1 Mrs D Power, Ascot House, London Road, Wrotham Heath, SEVENOAKS, Kent, TN15 7TB
2 Miss K Burns, 15 Hamilton Road, TUNBRIDGE WELLS, Kent, TN1 1LB

UNIT 4   MOTEL

1 Mr and Mrs V Down, Bridge House, South Park, LINCOLN, LN5 8ES
2 King Lighting Company Limited, 6–12 William Street, MAIDENHEAD, Berks, SL4 1AY
3 Editor, District News, 18 Stane Street, WINDSOR, Berks SL4 1AY

UNIT 5   SOLICITOR

1 Mr Walter North, 6 Parkway, Dulwich, LONDON, SE21 7JP
2 Mrs K Love, Willow Farm, BEMBRIDGE, Isle of Wight, PO35 5PR
3 Mr and Mrs R White, 14 Colmore Grove, EPSOM, Surrey, KT17 4QF

UNIT 6   CAMPING MAGAZINE

1 Miss G Bond, 2 Lodge Drive, Silsden, KEIGHLEY, W Yorkshire, BD20 9LP

UNIT 7   BUILDING CONTRACTOR

1 Wright & Long Limited, 156 Broad Street, BIRMINGHAM, B3 2QQ

3 Mrs D West, Horton House, Low Hill, HALESOWEN, W Midlands, B62 8BP

4 Mr D Redman, 32a Queen's Drive, BIRMINGHAM, B33 0TB

UNIT 8   EXHIBITION CENTRE

1 Mr Mark Steel, 4 Egerton Road, SHEFFIELD, S1 4JX

UNIT 9   PUBLISHER

1 Mrs Pamela Hall, Trellis House, Stoney Stanton Road, COVENTRY, Warks, CV6 5GT

2 Miss D Field, 9 Gresham Court, Manor Road, Filton, BRISTOL, BS12 7QE

3 Mr J Waterman, Plough Cottage, Cider Lane, HEREFORD, HR4 0LE

4 Mr P Grade and Mr H Young, 17 Hill Street, Horbury, WAKEFIELD, W Yorkshire, WF4 5QH

UNIT 10   LOCAL GOVERNMENT

1 Mr Colin Sell, 52 Woodlea Rise, Tollesbury, MALDON, Essex, CM9 8XD

4 Advertising Manager, District Journal, 6 Market Square, CHELMSFORD, Essex, CM1 3BH

UNIT 11   TRAVEL CONSULTANTS

1 Head Postmaster, 114 High Street, ST ALBANS, Herts, AL1 5UF

4 Miss Ann Test, Flat 5, Ashley Court, Masons Hill, BERKHAMPSTED, Herts, HP4 2ST

UNIT 13   HOSPITAL

1 Mr J Friend, 8 Station Parade, SIDCUP, Kent, DA15 7BJ

3 Mr Terry Wood, King's School, Dunton Road, LONDON, N16 0RH

UNIT 14   SHIPPING AGENT

2 Mr T Freeman, 39 Fairview Gardens, NEW MILTON, Hants, BH25 6QS

UNIT 15 INSURANCE BROKER

1 Miss May Bond, 5 Brook Crescent, WALTON–ON–THAMES, Surrey, KT12 2QS

UNIT 16 DEPARTMENT STORE

1 Mrs J Grain, 23 Royston Terrace, EDINBURGH, EH4 3EU
3 Mrs P Manners, Peter House, New Road, THURSO, Caithness, KW14 7TZ

UNIT 17 RESIDENTS' ASSOCIATION

3 Mr S Page, 47 Croft Avenue, WORTHING, Sussex, BN11 2DY

UNIT 18 BANK AREA OFFICE

1 Mr R Sweet, Brick Kiln Works, Tapps Lane, Plympton, PLYMOUTH, Devon, PL7 4SH
2 Mr David Long, 12 Bank Chambers, Silver Street, EXETER, Devon, EX2 9JY
3 Mr and Mrs R Booker, 4 Abbots Close, NEWTON ABBOT, Devon, TQ12 6QD
4 Mr R Price, Company Secretary, Gold & Masters Ltd, 18 Jarvis House, TOTNES, Devon, TQ9 5AL

UNIT 19 STATIONERS

1 Messrs W R Worth & Sons, 133 High Street, HEXHAM, Northumberland, NE46 4RP
2 Lines Typewriter Accessories Ltd, 45 Roundhay Industrial Estate, CRAMLINGTON, Northumberland, NE23 6EU
3 Messrs G R Marks & Company, Insurance Brokers, 269 Commercial Street, NEWCASTLE UPON TYNE, NE5 1LD
4 Quick-Work Printers Ltd, 2 Station Yard, MORPETH, Northumberland, NE61 4PE

UNIT 20 AUDIO–VISUAL AIDS

1 Mr B Cryer, 5 City House, Roman Street, NORWICH, Norfolk, NR5 0AB
2 Mr C Strange, 26 Rivermill Road, HITCHIN, Herts, SG5 1LA
3 Messrs Storey & Watcham, 2–16 Torr Place, LONDON, WC2N 6EZ
4 Mrs E Yardley, High Ridge, Hillborough, CAMBRIDGE, CB5 9EJ

UNIT 1 *Electricity Board*

You are working for the Manager of the Valley District Office.

1 LETTER TO MR W BLACK

New words: meter, Yours faithfully

Mr W Black, Dear Sir, (*Heading*) FINAL NOTICE. Recently we sent / you a bill for £40.80 in respect of / the electricity you have used up to the last meter / reading. From our records it seems that you have not / yet paid this bill. If this is so will you / please let us have payment within seven days from the / date of this letter. If you do not pay within / this time for the electricity used we may have to / cut off your supply. Unfortunately this will cost you at / least £6 to have the supply connected again and / you will of course still have to pay the outstanding / bill. We may also ask for a deposit before making / another connection to the electricity supply. We do not wish / to have to take this course of action and hope / to receive your cheque in full settlement by return. Yours / faithfully

(151 words, 1.37 SI)

2 DRAFT EXTRACT FOR A LEAFLET

New words: select, vouchers, stamps, stick

(*Heading*) EASY WAYS TO PAY YOUR ELECTRICITY BILL. In winter most / people use more electricity and so their bills are heavier? / It is sometimes difficult to find sufficient ready money to / meet these heavy bills. One of our easy payment plans / might help to ease the problem as they average out / the cost more evenly throughout the year. You can select / from the following: 1. Paying in equal monthly instalments by / standing order through your bank. 2. Paying in equal monthly / payments to your electricity showroom using our special vouchers. 3. / Buying 50p savings stamps from your electricity showroom. You / can buy as many as you like as often as / you like and stick them on a special card. You / then use them to help pay your bill. If you / would like further details of these arrangements please write to / us or call in at any of our showrooms for / an application form. We shall be happy to discuss any / problems with you.

(163 words, 1.45 SI)

1

3 CIRCULAR LETTER TO CONSUMERS

80 3/86

New words: consumer, efficiency, useful

Dear Consumer, In our notice at the end of May / we stated that there would be increases in our electricity / charges. The higher costs of coal and oil used in / the production of electricity, together with other items, have made / these increases necessary. The new charges apply to the first / normal meter reading date after 30 June. This means that / the bill enclosed with this letter is most likely to / be your first at the new rates. We hope you / will settle this bill promptly as this helps us to / keep our basic costs down and improve the efficiency of / our service. It is not possible for us to continue / supplying electricity if consumers do not pay their bills but / we may be able to help you if you are / in difficulty provided you contact us early enough. For your / information we enclose details of the various ways in which / you could pay your bill and we hope this leaflet / may be useful to you. Yours faithfully

(167 words, 1.45 SI)

4 LETTER TO MRS STANTON

70 3/86

New words: Mrs, Stanton, Madam, appliances

Mrs R Stanton, Dear Madam, With regard to your letter / dated yesterday we are pleased to send you a copy / of our notes on SAVING ELECTRICITY IN THE HOME. The / most common electrical appliances found in a modern home are / listed in these notes together with an approximate number of / units used in an average week. We also give the / maximum number of hours that each appliance can be used / for just one unit of electricity. For example, an iron / burns only one unit for every two hours that it / is used. The notes include several methods of saving power / and we are sure you will find our advice helpful / in reducing your bills. It is a good idea to / keep a record of your meter readings on a frequent / and regular basis so that you can see if your / savings plan is being effective. We are happy to have / been of service to you. Yours faithfully

(157 words, 1.43 SI)

UNIT 2 *Building Society*

You are working in a Branch Office of the Wideopen Building Society and have been asked to take dictation from the Manager (Tom Haynes) while his secretary is on sick leave.

1 MEMORANDUM TO DENNIS SOUTH

New words: Dennis, James, central

(*To*) Dennis South, Head Office (*Heading*) ADVANCE ON MORTGAGE. I attach an / application received yesterday from Mr James Strong. He is asking / for an advance against his present mortgage account to cover / the cost of a new central heating system. Mr Strong / has made all his payments promptly and I can recommend / this loan.

(52 words, 1.52 SI)

2 LETTER TO MISS SALLY DAY

New words: Sally, Yours sincerely

Miss Sally Day, Dear Miss Day, I have received your / letter of 10 June enclosing your pass book and cheque / in respect of last month's mortgage account. I see that / you have not signed the cheque so I am returning / it to you together with your pass book. Would you / please sign the cheque and return it promptly with the / pass book as soon as possible so that I can / credit your account before the end of this month which / will save you extra interest charges? Yours sincerely

(88 words, 1.28 SI)

3 DRAFT LETTER FOR DUPLICATING

New words: agency, lunch, withdrawals, enquiries, efficiently, parking

Dear Customer, We are very pleased to announce that we / are opening a new agency in your area at number / 23 High Street. From Monday to Friday the opening / hours will be 9 am to 5 pm / and we shall close for lunch from 1 to 2 / pm. This should make it easier than ever for / you to use all the various services we offer. Our / new agency will be able to provide a full service / for deposits and

3

withdrawals on any of our accounts. We / can assure you that our staff will be pleased to / receive your enquiries and deal with them quickly and efficiently. / If it is convenient for you why not call in / to see us at 23 High Street where we / have good car parking facilities? It is hoped that you / will find our new agency useful and we look forward / to being of service to you. Yours faithfully

(158 words, 1.46 SI)

4 CIRCULAR LETTER TO THE SHAREHOLDERS

New words: situated, voting, election, attend, society

Dear Shareholder, We have pleasure in enclosing a copy of / the Report and Financial Statements for the last year, issued / by our Board for distribution to all members. You will / appreciate that even in the present extremely difficult situation we / have been successful in improving our services which are available / to the public. One big step forward has been the / opening of four new Branch Offices, all situated in the / north of the country, where previously we have had very / few offices. This would not have been possible without the / co-operation of management and staff who have worked together for / the common good. We also enclose notice of the Annual / General Meeting and your voting paper for the election of / four new directors. You do of course have the right / to attend the AGM and vote at the / Meeting. You will be required to produce your pass book / or other record of your membership of the Society. Please / note that each member is allowed only one vote no / matter how many accounts he or she holds. If we / can be of any further help to you please do / not hesitate to get in touch with us in this / office. Yours faithfully

(203 words, 1.49 SI)

5 LETTER TO MR JAMES STRONG

Mr James Strong, Dear Mr Strong, I acknowledge receipt of / your application for an advance against your present mortgage account / and have submitted this to my Head Office for their / consideration. I do not expect any difficulty over this request / as the reason you require the money is entirely acceptable. / However, you should not go forward with the work until / you receive confirmation in writing that the sum applied for / has been finally approved. It might be as long as / ten days before I hear the result of your application / but if it is agreed a cheque will be forwarded / to you without any further delay. Yours sincerely

(108 words, 1.57 SI)

UNIT 3 *Garden Centre*

You are secretary to the Manager, Barry Mills, of the Green Fingers Garden Centre.

90
27/5/86

1 LETTER TO MRS D POWER

New words: bulbs, satisfaction, bonemeal

Mrs D Power, Dear Madam, We acknowledge receipt of your / large order for bulbs which were advertised as a special / offer recently. As agreed they will be delivered to you / by our own truck, cash on delivery, within the next / week. We are certain that our bulbs will give complete / satisfaction as we feel that the quality is better than / ever this year. It has always been our custom to / guarantee that if any of our bulbs do not grow / into beautiful plants we will replace them or return your / money in full. This guarantee remains in force for a / whole year after we have supplied the goods. In reply / to your request for a quantity of bonemeal we can / supply this in 7, 28 and 56 lb / sizes. Our catalogue and current price list covering this / item is enclosed and we shall be pleased to hear / by return if you require a supply of bonemeal to / be included with your bulb order. We look forward to / receiving your further instructions. Yours faithfully

(176 words, 1.41 SI)

2 LETTER TO MISS K BURNS

New words: improvements, garden, flower, paths, measurements

Miss K Burns, Dear Miss Burns, We are pleased to / hear that you are planning improvements to your property and / that a friend of yours has specially recommended us as / experts in garden design. It is noted that in the / first instance you would like us to design a large / water garden to cover an area behind your house which / is at present covered by flower beds and concrete paths, / and to include a section for fish and a small / waterfall. Before we can proceed with a design and quotation / for your consideration we should like our representative, Mr Brake, / to visit the site to discuss your requirements more fully. / He will need to take specific ground measurements and to / see how far the water supply needs to be piped. / Accordingly we have asked Mr Brake to telephone you next / week to arrange a convenient time to call on you. / Yours sincerely

(152 words, 1.43 SI)

3 EXTRACT FOR A LEAFLET

New words: carefully, sunshine, dry, draughts, damp, spray

(*Heading*) CARING FOR YOUR HOUSE PLANTS. Before you decide on buying / your house plants it is suggested that you study carefully / their particular requirements. Most plants need sunshine if they are / to produce good growth and many need special care. Make / sure you are able to provide the correct conditions for / the house plants you will be purchasing. New plants take / time to get used to a new home and they / may lose a few leaves or stop growing for a / little while. Give them a good drink of water if / they are dry when you get them home. Use water / that has been brought to room heat and then leave / the plants in a warm place. Plants need air but / certainly not draughts or extremes of heat or cold. A / window that opens at the top is best. Daylight is / important to plants for full growth but electric lighting can / be used. It is a good idea to stand your / plants on a bed of damp stones which will help / to keep them healthy. A light spray applied not too / frequently also helps to keep most plants in good condition. / Plants sold through retail outlets usually have care-notes attached / to them. It is wise to follow the instructions given / if you want to grow beautiful plants to add colour / to your home.

(223 words, 1.27 SI)

4 NOTICE TO ALL STAFF

New words: specialist, practice

(*To*) All Staff (*Heading*) SPECIALIST STAFF TRAINING. As a member of / staff of a specialist company such as ours you are / frequently asked questions on gardening matters. We wish to provide / the best possible service for our customers in this respect / and we have therefore arranged a number of training programmes / for all our employees. These will take the form of / short courses and 'on site' visits designed to teach as / wide a knowledge as possible of all kinds of garden / work. Full details of dates and subject areas will be / issued soon. In the immediate future we plan to extend / our training programme in the management field for employees who / have been with us over 5 years. We shall continue / our practice whenever possible of promoting managers from within our / organisation.

(131 words, 1.46 SI)

UNIT 4 *Motel*

You are working for Basil Lock, proprietor of the Top Grade Motel.

1 LETTER TO MR AND MRS V DOWN

New words: expensive, dining-room, bars, Motel

Mr and Mrs V Down, Dear Mr and Mrs Down, / Thank you for your telephone call asking for rooms for / yourselves and also for your mother and father for the / last weekend in April. I understand that your brother is / getting married then, so you will also require an additional / room for him for just one night. I have a / large family unit available which would provide three bedrooms with / a shared sitting-room. This unit would be less expensive / than taking three separate units and I am sending you / details of our prices and a booking form. I would / point out that our dining-room offers an excellent meals / service all week but on Sundays we serve lunches only. / During permitted opening hours we serve light meals in both / the Motel bars. I hope to receive your completed booking / form in due course and assure you of our attention / at all times. Yours sincerely

(155 words, 1.42 SI)

2 LETTER TO KING LIGHTING COMPANY LIMITED

New words: advertisement, automatically, enter, computer, economical, modernised

King Lighting Company Limited, Dear Sirs, I have seen your / advertisement in the local paper offering free advice on lighting / arrangements and would like you to survey our premises. At / the present time the Motel is being modernised and I / wish to improve the lighting in our units and public / rooms. I am also thinking of installing a control system / for the units which will allow lights to go on / and off automatically when people enter or leave the rooms, / thus effecting the maximum saving of electricity. Therefore, if you / are experienced in the various types of computer controlled systems / which are on the market, I should like you to / submit details of a system which would be both simple / to operate and economical to use. I look forward to / hearing from you shortly on these matters. Yours faithfully

(139 words, 1.56 SI)

3 LETTER TO THE EDITOR, DISTRICT NEWS

New words: editor, eat, dancing, selection, specialities, features

The Editor, District News, Dear Sir, I understand that you / are running a weekly item on local places in which / to eat out and I wonder whether you are aware / of the facilities offered by this Motel for dining and / dancing. We have one of the largest and best dining- / rooms in the area and we offer a wide selection / of English food including many specialities. We also offer a / business lunch from Monday to Friday at a very reasonable / price. In addition there is a separate dining area that / can be booked for parties. I should be happy if / your features writer would lunch here with me so that / we could talk about a suitable advertisement to go with / any coverage you may offer this Motel. May I suggest / Tuesday next week at 1 pm as a convenient / day to meet? If you agree to this arrangement would / you please ask your representative to telephone me to confirm / the time? Yours faithfully

(164 words, 1.49 SI)

4 MEMORANDUM TO MOTEL HOUSEKEEPER

New words: housekeeper, complaints, towels, bathmat, tear, soaps

(*To*) Motel Housekeeper, I have had a few complaints recently about / the standard of service in our units. Customers have made / the following observations: 1. The house rule calling for two / small and two large towels per person, plus one bathmat / per unit, has not always been carried out. 2. Old / sheets have been used which tear easily. 3. Self-service / items are not stocked up regularly and soaps are sometimes / in short supply. These complaints are serious matters for the / motel. Please instruct your staff to pay particular attention to / the items mentioned above as we cannot allow the standard / of service to fall. Competition has increased lately and we / must maintain high standards of efficiency if we are to / remain in business. As a result of these complaints will / you please check your inventory as I wish to have / an indication of how many replacements you estimate will be / required during the next quarter.

(155 words, 1.50 SI)

UNIT 5 *Solicitor*

You are working for Mr Henry Carr of Carr & Page, Solicitors.

1 LETTER TO MR WALTER NORTH

New words: Walter, Pan, profitable, London

Mr Walter North, Dear Walter, I was pleased to receive / your letter
of 2 November requesting me to act on / your behalf in the purchase
of 500 £1 / shares in the Pan Oil Company. I confirm that the / shares
have now been purchased and duly registered in your / name. I have
forwarded my agent's contract by registered mail / to your bank in
accordance with your instructions. Your bank / will then be able to
charge your account with the / total cost of the shares as per copy
enclosed. I / am glad to have acted for you in this instance / and I feel
certain that our agent has made a / profitable purchase for you
although this was quite difficult in / the present market situation. No
doubt I will see you / at the Law Association's meeting next Saturday
in London. Yours / sincerely

(141 words, 1.42 SI)

2 LETTER TO MRS K LOVE

New words: aunt, Jane, divided, Sydney, Australia, vacant

Mrs K Love, Dear Madam, We are acting on behalf / of your aunt,
Jane Young, who died last month. Under / the terms of her Will her
estate is to be / divided between yourself and your brother. At the
moment we / have been unable to contact your brother at the address /
given to us of 44 Lower Road, Sydney, Australia / 2096 and we should
be glad if / you could assist us in locating him. You are probably /
aware that your aunt's estate includes two properties in London / and
in accordance with her wishes these are to be / sold and the proceeds
are to be divided between yourself / and your brother. We have asked
a local agent to / value the properties and they have estimated each to
be / worth approximately £60,000. We do not expect any / difficulty
in obtaining this price quite quickly for either property / as both
houses are vacant and in excellent order. We / trust you can help us to
contact your brother in / Australia so that we can proceed to carry out
the / terms of your late aunt's Will. Yours faithfully

(188 words, 1.43 SI)

9

3 LETTER TO MR AND MRS R WHITE

New words: drawn, preparing, specified

Mr and Mrs R White, Dear Mr and Mrs White / (*Heading*) NO 2 MILL CLOSE. Following our meeting with you both / last week we have drawn up an Agreement covering the / field at the back of your house at the above / address which you propose to lease for training horses. A / copy of this Agreement has been forwarded to the interested / party for his comments. We do not expect any delay / in preparing a lease once the Agreement has been signed / and returned to us. It will be a short-term / lease and the Local Authority has already given approval for / the land to be used for the purpose specified in / the Agreement. We will be in touch as soon as / we have further news for you. Yours sincerely

(128 words, 1.40 SI)

4 LETTER TO CHIEF TOWN PLANNING OFFICER

New words: officer, extension, already, objection, surveyor

Chief Town Planning Officer, Dear Sir, (*Heading*) PROPOSED EXTENSION AT 6 / RIVER WAY. I am representing Mr James East of 8 / River Way in the above matter. He informs me that / he has not received any written notice of a proposed / extension to 6 River Way but has seen reference to / it in the local paper. As the property is next / door to his own he has seen the plans at / your office and finds that the proposed extension will considerably / reduce the daylight to his west facing rooms. On these / grounds he is against the proposal and has already informed / your office of his objection. Mr East will be overseas / on business for the next six months and wishes me / to meet your surveyor when he next visits the site / to discuss the proposed extension far more fully. I shall / be pleased to hear from you on this matter. Yours / faithfully

(151 words, 1.42 SI)

UNIT 6 *Camping Magazine*

You are secretary to the Editor of *Camping for All*.

1 LETTER TO MISS G BOND

New words: camping, favourite, deadline, photographs, Republic, Germany

Miss G Bond, Dear Miss Bond, In the February issue / of *Camping for All* I plan to run a feature / about some of our regular writers' favourite camping sites. The / deadline for copy is 3rd January and I should be / very glad indeed if you could let me have approximately / 600 to 700 words about your favourite camping / site. Please say why this particular site interests you so / much and state when you last paid a visit to / it. Also tell us of any major changes that have / taken place since you were there previously. If possible I / should like you to send me at least three black / and white or coloured photographs. Am I right in thinking / that you will be going to the Federal Republic of / Germany again this year? On your return why not send / me a piece of about 2000 words together with / several good photographs? Yours sincerely

(155 words, 1.44 SI)

2 COMPETITION FEATURE

New words: holiday, circle, entry, prize, Amsterdam, Paris

(Heading) HOLIDAY COMPETITION. All you have to do to enter for / this competition is to study the two pictures marked A / and B and put a circle around the 10 differences / you can discover in Drawing B. Fill in your name / and address on the form given below and send your / entry back to *Camping for All* to reach us no / later than 31 March. The first prize is a / free return trip for four people to Amsterdam and the / second prize is a free return trip for two people / to Paris to be taken before 31 December this / year. Do remember to make sure that your entry is / sent in in good time and that you have put / your correct name and address in full.

(127 words, 1.34 SI)

3 RULES FOR HOLIDAY COMPETITION

New words: awarded, winners, published, entered

(Heading) RULES FOR THE HOLIDAY COMPETITION. 1. No employee of the / Company is allowed to enter for the competition. 2. All / forms must be received by 31 March. 3. The / first correct entry to be opened after 31 March / will be awarded the first prize and the second correct / entry will be given the second prize. 4. Both winners / will be informed by phone by 15 April and the / names of the winners will be published in the May / issue of *Camping for All*. 5. The judge's decision must / be accepted as final and no correspondence can be entered / into.

(101 words, 1.46 SI)

4 DISPLAYED NOTICE

New words: practical, exhibition, Manchester, bargains

The March issue of *Camping for All* will be on / sale from 20 February and as usual it will be / full of interesting and practical features. Special items will include / a review of the camping holiday exhibition to be held / in Manchester at the end of the month; an appraisal / of new camping equipment which has recently come on to / the market; and some excellent second-hand sale bargains. All / this plus our regular features of 'Round the UK / sites', 'News and views on camping', 'The Women's page' and / 'Holiday suggestions'. Have you yet placed a regular order for / *Camping for All*? If not, why not do so now?

(110 words, 1.48 SI)

5 EDITORIAL

New words: abroad, Europe, preliminary, article

Now is the time to make your plans for this / year's camping season. We know that many of you go / camping abroad but some of our readers may be thinking / about driving to other parts of Europe for the very / first time. With a little careful thought and attention to / detail this can be a wonderful experience. Do make sure / that you read our helpful article on page 15 on / 'Your first camping holiday abroad'. It gives a lot of / very practical advice and help. We should be happy if / you would write to us when you return and share / some of your unusual experiences on camp sites abroad. We / will pay £10 for any letters received from you / which we print on this subject. We hope you have / a lovely holiday wherever you go, in this country or / overseas. Bill Friend

(143 words, 1.38 SI)

UNIT 7 *Building Contractor*

You are working for the Managing Director, John Carter, of John Carter & Co Ltd.

1 LETTER TO WRIGHT & LONG LIMITED

Wright & Long Limited, Dear Sirs, I am in receipt / of your letter of 2 January asking us to give / you a quotation for painting the outside of your firm's / main building and replacing the missing glass in a number / of windows in your factory. We have surveyed the two / premises and attach our specification setting out in detail the / work we consider necessary for each property. As you require / the work to be completed within the next month we / must have your decision without delay so that we can / reserve sufficient men for the whole contract. Yours faithfully

(99 words, 1.52 SI)

2 MEMORANDUM TO HARRY MANN, COMPANY SECRETARY

New words: Harry, Secretary

(*To*) Harry Mann, Company Secretary (*Heading*) CENTRAL HEATING INSTALLATION. Re the above, / I am returning the two copies of our new Maintenance / Agreement from our usual firm to cover the next three / years and agree that the annual charge appears to be / very high for the amount of extra work involved. It / would be as well for us to attempt to get a / few more quotations, perhaps from small local firms, as I / consider that we do not always get quite the same / personal service from larger organisations. It would also be in / our own interests to build up good connections with a / local central heating engineer as we might be able to / help each other out in various ways. Kindly let me / know the moment you get more information.

(127 words, 1.50 SI)

3 LETTER TO MRS D WEST

New words: satisfied, surface, weather, locality

Mrs D West, Dear Mrs West, I am interested to / learn that your friend, Mrs Foot, has strongly recommended us / to you because she is so completely satisfied with the / new front drive we have just constructed at her home. / We shall be pleased to quote you for similar work / though initially it would be advisable for me to call / upon you to measure up your drive and have a discussion / with you as to the most suitable type of surface / for us to use. I can then take measurements of / the area involved and let you have an estimate for / materials and labour. However, I regret that we should not / be able to start working on your drive before the / end of March. In any case it would not be / wise to begin work until the winter is over as / there will be a better chance then to complete the / job quickly if the weather is good. I shall be / in your locality next Thursday afternoon and I will phone / you before then to check whether it will be a / suitable time to call. Yours sincerely

(186 words, 1.38 SI)

4 LETTER TO MR D REDMAN

Mr D Redman, Dear Sir, Further to my visit last / week I have now prepared plans for the extension you / propose for your property. I confirm that planning permission will / be required from the Local Authority and we will arrange / for the plans to be submitted to them on your / behalf in due course. There are one or two small / points which need your consideration before I complete the plans / and estimate for the job. The new building line will / extend 12 ft into your garden area and in order / to put in the footings we will have to take / down your summer-house. Do you wish us to estimate / for this job also? It is recommended that you move / a number of plants before construction work can begin and / it might be more satisfactory from your point of view / if an expert from a garden centre were to carry / out this work. Please let me have your observations on / these matters as soon as you possibly can. Yours faithfully /

(170 words, 1.39 SI)

UNIT 8 Exhibition Centre

You are secretary to the Manager of the GB Exhibition Centre.

1 PERSONAL LETTER TO MR MARK STEEL

New words: private, admitted

Mr Mark Steel, Dear Mark, When you were here on / a flying visit two months ago you asked me to / send you some general data about the next large art / exhibition we will be holding at our Centre. It has / now been decided to schedule this for November of next / year and it will be open for private showings on / Tuesday and Wednesday, 6th and 7th November from 1100 / to 1600 hours. The public will be admitted for / the rest of that week and for the whole of / the following three weeks from 0900 to 1800 / hours. This is just advance information for you as I / knew that you wished to keep a day free but / there may of course be some last minute changes. I / will send you the brochure as soon as it is / produced. With all good wishes, Yours sincerely

(147 words, 1.32 SI)

2 MEMORANDUM TO ALL STAFF

New words: badges, communication, visitors, wears, security

(*To*) All Staff (*Heading*) INDIVIDUAL BADGES. To assist communication at the Motor / Show in October arrangements have been
made for special coloured / badges to be issued. Our own staff will
have their / usual gold ones, UK visitors will be given blue / ones and
our overseas visitors will have red badges. Please / make sure that
every person attending the Show wears a / badge at all times. This will
be of particular help / to the security staff.

(74 words, 1.50 SI)

3 NOTES

New words: desks, telex, halls, exit

(*Main heading*) NOTES OF GENERAL INFORMATION FOR
THE ANNUAL BOOK MARKET FROM / 24–28 SEPTEMBER.
(*Side heading*) Hours—The Market is / open on Wednesday 24th and
Thursday 25th September / from 0900 to 1800 and on Friday 26th
September / from 0900 to 1600. (*Side heading*) *Working Office for* /
Visitors—There will be an official centre for any visitors / who require
an office in which to work. It will / be fully equipped with desks,
telephones, telex and word processing / machines. A small charge will
be made for the use / of the office and special passes will be required.
(*Side heading*) *Telephones*/—There are four public telephones in each of
the two / Halls near the exit. (*Side heading*) *Stands*—The dealers' stands
are located / as follows: Hall A, ground floor, stand numbers one to /
ninety-nine; Hall A, first floor, stand numbers one hundred / to one
hundred and ninety-nine; Hall B, ground floor, / stand numbers two
hundred to two hundred and ninety-nine / and Hall B, first floor,
stand numbers three hundred to / three hundred and ninety-nine.

(175 words, 1.45 SI)

4 PRESS NOTICE

New words: exhibiting, films, exact

The Exhibition Centre is holding its third Annual Business Show / all
next week from Monday, 3rd August to Friday, 7th / August when
over 300 firms will be exhibiting. The / varied programme of events
will include some special staff training / films which will be shown
free of charge at various / times throughout the whole week. A full list
of the / films is available on request from the Manager of the / Centre.
The drawing given below shows the location of the / Centre and gives
the position of the two large car / parking areas which are directly
outside the main building.

(99 words, 1.47 SI)

UNIT 9 *Publisher*

You are working for the Senior Editor in Little's Educational Publishing House.

1 LETTER TO MRS PAMELA HALL

New words: Pamela, specimen, manuscript, despatch

Mrs Pamela Hall, Dear Pamela, Thank you so much for / agreeing to read the sample material for the proposed book / entitled 'Earning a Living'. I am enclosing 25 specimen / pages of the work and also one of our standard / reviewer's report forms for your specific comments. I look forward / to hearing your opinion of this manuscript and to receiving / your report. I shall be on holiday until 29th / July so perhaps you would be good enough to despatch / the work so that it will reach me early in / August. Yours sincerely

(93 words, 1.54 SI)

2 LETTER TO MISS D FIELD

New words: author's, hardback, softback, encouraging

Miss D Field, Dear Miss Field, I was sorry to / hear from my secretary this afternoon that you had telephoned / my office earlier today to say that the six author's / copies of your new book have not yet arrived at / your address. I immediately spoke to Mr Major who is / in charge of our warehouse and discovered that they have / been having some difficulty with their computer and all deliveries / of books have been delayed. However, the new books have / now been despatched and I have asked him to make / sure that six copies of your book are sent to / you as quickly as possible so I hope they will / be with you very soon now. I do apologise for / the long delay. The book does seem to be selling / well and I believe that sales and orders up to / the end of last week were nearly a thousand for / the hardback and five thousand for the softback. This is / most encouraging as the book has been on the market / for only nine weeks. Yours sincerely

(176 words, 1.35 SI)

3 LETTER TO MR J WATERMAN

New words: remainder, option

Mr J Waterman, Dear Mr Waterman (*Heading*) ANIMALS ON THE FARM. / We very much regret that the sales of the above / children's

16

book have fallen below the level at which it / is economic for us to continue to stock the book / and list it in our catalogue. Therefore it is our / wish to remainder the stock and we have received an / offer of 50p per copy. We need your approval / for this procedure under the terms of our contract with / you and you have the option of receiving 12 free / copies or of buying a larger number of copies at / the remainder price of 50p. We should be glad / if you would let us have your decision within 14 / days from the date of this letter. Yours sincerely

(129 words, 1.41 SI)

4 LETTER TO MR P GRADE AND MR H YOUNG

New words: reprint, revising, edition, revision

Mr P Grade and Mr H Young, Dear Mr Grade / and Mr Young, (*Heading*) LABORATORY TRAINING FOR SCHOOLS. I am pleased / to tell you that the sales of your book have / gone so well that we have just taken a fourth / reprint of it of 3000 copies. In view of / the very successful sales of this book I should like / to make the suggestion that you consider the possibility of / revising it for a new edition which we would hope / to put on the market in the summer or winter / of next year. On looking through this book it seems to me that / there might be a good case for a revision of / units four, five, eight and eleven but you may welcome / the opportunity to rewrite others. Would you please be kind / enough to let me know what you think about this? / With best wishes, Yours sincerely

(145 words, 1.36 SI)

UNIT 10 *Local Government*

You are working for Mary Piper, Chief Personnel Officer.

1 LETTER TO MR COLIN SELL

New words: Colin, accountant, applicants, vacancy

Mr Colin Sell, Dear Mr Sell, Your letter of application / for the position of assistant accountant which was published in / last month's *Local Government News* has been passed to me / for reply. I regret very much that your application arrived / here too late for you to be considered for the / short list of applicants and I am sorry that the /

vacancy has now been filled. However, there is a similar / position becoming vacant next month which is in the Accounts / Department of one of our district offices. I am enclosing / details of this new vacancy along with an application form / should you wish to apply for this new job. Yours / sincerely

(111 words, 1.52 SI)

2 MEMORANDUM TO ALL DEPARTMENTAL MANAGERS

New words: departmental, necessarily, attendance

(To) All Departmental Managers *(Heading)* FURTHER EDUCATION COURSES. Courses start in September / and I have been requested to draw your attention to / our policy which allows all employees who are under the / age of 18 to spend one day per week on / an F.E. Course. The course decided upon does not / necessarily have to cover a subject area which is connected / with their employment. Will you please let me know the / names of any new members of your staff who wish / to attend an F.E. course next September and whether / they wish to take a course near their home or / their work place? I also need to know if there / are any members of your staff still under the age / of 18 who wish to continue for a second year / of their part-time course. Please note that attendance for / a second year is only agreed if a satisfactory report / has been received on the first year's study. Kindly let / me have your list of names by the end of / this week.

(172 words, 1.38 SI)

3 MEMORANDUM TO MEDICAL OFFICER

(To) Medical Officer, *(Heading)* DAY CENTRE. At the Management Meeting today I / was told by your Chief Assistant that the Day Centre / Manager will be leaving in a month's time because he / has been in poor health for some time and that / you are going to advertise the vacancy as soon as / possible. Before I proceed with this matter I should like / to have your confirmation that the existing job details are / correct and that you will not be wishing to change / them in any way at all. If you do decide / to change any area of responsibility for this job you / will of course have to get the approval of your / Management Committee which meets only once a month. It would / be advisable to review the job specification quickly and let / me know if there are any changes to be made. /

(140 words, 1.43 SI)

18

4 LETTER TO ADVERTISING MANAGER, DISTRICT JOURNAL

New words: Journal, alone, holder

Advertising Manager, District Journal, Dear Sir, We give below copy / of an advertisement we should like to appear in the / next issue of your paper. Please use our established design / and size: 'A vacancy exists in the Town Planning Officer's / Department for a Personal Assistant. The job would suit a / person who has good office experience and can work under / pressure. The successful applicant must be able to work alone / and not object to a very varied volume of work. / He or she will be expected to answer directly to / the Town Planning Officer. The position is now vacant because / the present holder has been promoted to another job. If / you would like to know more about the position send / full details of your education and past work experience to / the Chief Personnel Officer at the Town Hall.' I note / that for a small extra fee an advertisement can be / put in all four local papers owned by your group. / Please arrange for this to be done and charge us / direct according to your usual custom. Yours faithfully

(178 words, 1.46 SI)

UNIT 11 *Travel Consultants*

You are working as secretary to the Manager of Sharpnell Travel Ltd.

1 LETTER TO HEAD POSTMASTER

New words: postmaster, envelope, eventually, destination, tickets, contained

Head Postmaster, Dear Sir, We are enclosing an envelope which / you will note was posted by us on 4th May. / It eventually arrived at its destination, 10 miles away on / 12th May. As you can see it was immediately posted / back to us as the air tickets which it contained / had been required for 8th May. You will realise that / this delay in the postal service did cause us a / great deal of trouble and money and lost us a / valued customer. We are becoming rather concerned at the increasing / length of time being taken in the handling of correspondence / and we shall be most interested to hear your comments / on this important matter. Yours faithfully

(116 words, 1.47 SI)

2 FORMAT FOR STANDARD LETTER

New words: overdue, oversight, strictly, reminders

For the attention of . . . Dear Sir or Madam, (*Heading*) OVERDUE ACCOUNT! / It would appear from our records that the amount of / is outstanding on your account. We feel certain that this / is actually just an oversight on your part and we / would ask you to settle the balance of this account / by return of post. Please note that our terms of / trading are strictly net and that payment of all accounts / must be made prior to the 15th of the month / following the date of your invoice. We regret having to / send reminders of this sort but you will appreciate that / we are forced to do so. Yours faithfully

(108 words, 1.37 SI)

3 PAMPHLET TO SCHOOLS AND COLLEGES

**New words: Rotterdam, departure, accommodation,
              harbour, Euromast, tower**

(*Heading*) EDUCATIONAL VISITS TO ROTTERDAM. Why not spend two days in / Rotterdam for a very special student's price of £30? / The dates of departure are: 22 June, 27 / July, 24 August, 21 September. The price includes / the following: 1. Air ticket on a scheduled service between / London and Rotterdam which leaves early on Friday morning and / returns on Saturday night. 2. First class accommodation in single / rooms with all meals. 3. A planned trip round the / harbour and a visit to the Euromast Space Tower for / a wonderful view over the city. A copy of the / full programme will be sent to all students when they / receive their travel documents. We advise you to make an / early registration—just complete the attached form and return it / as soon as possible to our London Sales Office.

(139 words, 1.51 SI)

4 PERSONAL LETTER TO MISS ANN TEST

**New words: Europe, pamphlet, explains, travel, sightseeing,
              Moscow**

Miss Ann Test, Dear Ann, When I met your mother / a day or two ago she said something about your / wanting to visit the USSR with your / brother for a holiday early next year. She asked me / if I would send you some information about booking such / a holiday and to let you know what health certificates / are required. I think she felt that there would be / a lot of regulations which would be different from those / in other parts of Europe but it is really not / very involved. I am sending you a detailed pamphlet which / explains all you need to know about booking accommodation, medical / requirements, travel documents, etc. It also gives you some notes / on sightseeing in Moscow. You can book directly with / the USSR Offices in London or Manchester / and the pamphlet gives the telephone numbers. However, unless you / wish to make your own arrangements I can of course / handle all this for you. Why not phone me when / you get this letter and I will arrange a suitable / time for you and your brother to come to talk / to me? Would it take a weight off your mother's / mind if she were to come too? Every good wish, / Sincerely

(211 words, 1.37 SI)

UNIT 12 *Manufacturer*

You are working for the Factory Manager of the Model Toy Manufacturing Company.

1 NOTICE TO ALL FACTORY STAFF

New words: **smoking, protective, clothing, worn, inflammable, cabinets**

(*To*) All Factory Staff (*Heading*) SAFETY REGULATIONS. In the interests of safety / the following are to be carried out at all times: / 1. No smoking on any part of the factory floor / at any time. 2. Protective clothing is to be worn / in all places of work. This will include the Research / Division. 3. No electric fires are to be used on / the premises. 4. Any damage to leads or equipment must / be reported to me at once. 5. Fire doors must / never be left open. 6. All inflammable materials must be / stored in steel cabinets. Factory Manager

(96 words, 1.51 SI)

2 MEMORANDUM TO PERSONNEL DEPARTMENT

New words: **junior, typist, memoranda, signature, messages, interview**

(*To*) Personnel Department. Would you please be kind enough to advertise / for a new junior secretary for me, or perhaps you / could

recommend a typist from another Department who is worthy / of promotion and who has a capacity for hard work? / Her main duties will be the typing of letters, reports, / memoranda, etc as required. She will submit all completed work / for my approval and signature in the usual way. She / will be asked to file all mail in accordance with / the firm's standard filing system. She will be responsible for / opening incoming mail and sending outgoing mail from the Department. / She will have to answer my phone as well as / her own and take messages for me when I am / in the factory. These are her normal duties but there / may be a few extra items from time to time. I / need a secretary rather urgently as the volume of work / in the factory seems to be increasing every day. So / please let me know if it is possible for you / to short-list several girls for interview at the end / of this week. Many thanks.

(185 words, 1.47 SI)

3 MEMORANDUM TO MANAGING DIRECTOR

New words: caught, raise, appealed, daughter, auctioned, Fair

(*To*) Managing Director. A paragraph in last week's local newspaper caught / my eye concerning a small child living on the industrial / estate close by our factory. The life of this poor / little girl is in danger as she has a very / serious heart condition. The editor of the paper seems determined / to raise the necessary dollars in order to send her / to the USA for specialist attention and he / has appealed for funds. This week's paper shows that the / local people have been particularly helpful and have apparently raised / half the money. Today I have discovered that the child / is the daughter of one of our own employees. Do / you think it would be possible for the Company to / give its support by offering some goods which could be / auctioned at next Monday's Bank Holiday Fair?

(137 words, 1.50 SI)

4 MEMORANDUM TO PAUL RIVERS, MANAGER OF THE RESEARCH DIVISION

New word: Paul

(*To*) Paul Rivers, Manager, Research Division. We have done extremely well / over the past six months and sales figures have been / in excess of what we expected. There appears to be / an ever increasing demand for our new train sets. However, / we are still using the original model and I think / we ought to consider the development of a new and / up-to-date product as 'this is the age of / the train!' I should be glad to have your comments. /

(80 words, 1.40 SI)

UNIT 13 *Hospital*

You are working for the Co-ordinator of the Information Centre at City Hospital—Mrs Olive Kent.

1 LETTER TO MR J FRIEND

New words: overseas, organised, draft, itinerary

Mr J Friend, Dear Sir, Your letter asking if you / can bring a group of overseas students to this hospital / has been passed to me for attention. I understand that / they are on a course which includes the management of / hospitals and as part of their study they would like / to see how this large English hospital is organised. I / shall be glad to arrange a visit for them early / next month and I attach a draft itinerary. Please let / me know if this programme suits your needs. I will / then complete the arrangements and confirm date and times by / return. I look forward to hearing from you soon. Yours / faithfully

(111 words, 1.47 SI)

2 ITINERARY TO ATTACH TO LETTER TO MR J FRIEND

New words: Chairman, coffee, frame, role, wards, tea

(*Heading*) VISIT TO CITY HOSPITAL—PROGRAMME. 1. Meet in the Hall / at 10 am. Welcome by the Chairman of the / Hospital Management Group. 2. Coffee in the Board Room. 3. / Film showing how the hospital is organised. 4. How we / use the main frame computer both for our medical records / and in the Supplies Unit. 5. Lunch. 6. Visit to / the Out-Patients Department. 7. The role of the Hospital / Information Centre. 8. Tea in the Common Room. 9. A / visit to several wards—subject to patients' needs. 10. How / the Radio Station is run by patients. 11. Meet in / the Hall. Members of the office staff and nurses will / be available to answer questions. Close at 5.00 pm. /

(120 words, 1.45 SI)

3 LETTER TO TERRY WOOD, KING'S SCHOOL

New words: Terry, Wood, intensive, aids

Terry Wood, King's School, Dear Terry, I have received your / letter dated 9 January asking for help with your school / project on the use

23

of computers in hospitals. I am / sending you a number of brochures which give details of / our various departments and include notes on their work and / the use of computers. In these brochures are several colour / pictures which I think you will find useful for your / project. I am sorry that we do not produce a / brochure just for our Computer Centre but you may be / interested to know that we have now put the following / types of work on the computer: staff pay, accounts, stock / control, records in respect of our patients in the Intensive / Care Unit and teaching aids. I hope that this information / will help you and I wish you every success with / your project. Yours sincerely

(144 words, 1.43 SI)

4 DRAFT LEAFLET

New words: waiting, treatment, stay, toilet, admission

(Heading) INFORMATION FOR PATIENTS. Your name has now been placed on / our official waiting list and as soon as we have / a free bed you will be asked to come in / to start your treatment. This information sheet is to help / you prepare for your stay. *(Sub heading)* *Admission* Please let us know / at once if for any reason you cannot come into / hospital on the date and at the time requested. When / you arrive go straight to the ward named and report / to the nurse in charge. She will show you your / bed and make sure you are settled in comfortably. As / storage space is very limited it is best to bring / a friend with you who can take away items you / will not need whilst you are in hospital. If you / have to bring young children into hospital you are most / welcome to remain with them until they feel at home. / *(Sub heading)* *Personal Items* Please bring your own night and toilet things. / There is a store here where small items can be / purchased should you find that you need anything extra. *(Sub heading)* *Safety* / Do not bring any items of great value with you / and only enough money to buy papers and sweets etc. / If you do have to bring any valuables please ask / the nurse in charge to arrange for their safe keeping. / It is important to bring any pension or allowance documents / and hand them to the nurse in charge. *(Sub heading)* *Visiting* Two / people only are allowed by your bedside at any one / time. Normal visiting hours are every day from 7 to / 8 pm and Saturday and Sunday afternoons from 3 / to 4 pm. *(Sub heading)* *Car Parking* We regret that there / are no spaces at the hospital for visitors' cars but / there is a large public car park within easy walking / distance of all wards.

(304 words, 1.29 SI)

UNIT 14 *Shipping Agent*

You are working for Norman Wise, Chief Clerk of East & Son (London) Ltd.

1 MEMORANDUM TO BARRY CASE, ACCOUNTS

New words: Barry, Liverpool, Lading

(*To*) Barry Case, Accounts (*Heading*) THE RED CAR COMPANY—FREIGHT ACCOUNTS. The / above Company advise us that Freight Accounts for shipments of / their cars can no longer be processed by their London / office. With effect from 1st May all Freight Accounts must / be sent to their Liverpool agents, marked for the attention / of the Manager, Credit Department. They have asked us to / put the following details on all our invoices: the reference / number of the Shipping Instruction, the vessel's name, and the / number and date of the Bill of Lading. For the / present, invoices should be mailed in the normal way. I / will let you know in due course whether a 'quick / payment by statement system' can be set up.

(118 words, 1.41 SI)

2 LETTER TO MR T FREEMAN

New words: Perth, Western, arrival, urgent

Mr T Freeman, Dear Sir, With reference to our telephone / conversation with you last week, we are now able to / confirm that we have today received all the documents to / permit us to ship the 3 cases containing your valuable / works of art and personal effects via MV 'State / Express' sailing 4th August to Perth. The cases are being / shipped f.o.b. to our agent in Western Australia / who will be responsible for clearing them through their customs. / Kindly inform us who will be available to sign for / these cases on arrival at our agent's warehouse and if / we should submit our invoice in respect of charges direct / to you. This matter is urgent and your early reply / will be much appreciated. Yours faithfully

(126 words, 1.51 SI)

3 REPORT TO THE CHAIRMAN OF THE BOARD

New words: zone, carriage, port, traffic, legal, description

(*To*) Chairman of the Board (*Heading*) NEW SHIPPING CONDITIONS AND FORMS. I / give below notes on the meeting held last

Friday: (*Sub heading*) <u>Conditions</u> / It has now been agreed by the main shipping lines / operating in the North Sea Zone that the new conditions / of carriage will no longer be printed on the back / of the shipping document. In future they will be printed / on a separate sheet. The same conditions can then be / used for both normal port-to-port traffic and door/-to-door traffic. In drawing up these new conditions special / notice has been taken of the fact that the same / legal principles do not apply in all zones. (*Sub heading*) <u>Forms</u> A / new form has been designed which leaves space for a / description of the goods to be given on the same / side as the conditions of carriage. The main advantage of / the form being printed on one side only is that / it can then be used with computer systems. The new / conditions of carriage will be referred to in the shipping / document and if a customer asks for a copy it / can be attached. It will be a requirement to attach / a copy to all long-term agreements. The new documents / will be printed soon and must be used from 1st / June next.

(202 words, 1.42 SI)

4 URGENT NOTICE

New words: discharging, cargo, packed, labelled, hazard

(*Heading*) DANGEROUS GOODS This is to give shippers advance notice of / some important changes that will come into effect on 1st / March, and will apply to all ships loading or discharging / cargo at UK ports. The shipper will be required / to provide documents and details for all merchandise in the / above group as follows: 1. A certificate which states the / nature of the goods and their class. 2. Confirmation that / the shipment is clearly marked, etc. 3. Where such goods / are part of a freight unit, for example contained in / a vehicle, the person in charge must state that they / are safely packed within the unit. 4. All cases must / be clearly marked with the correct name of the goods / and properly labelled as to the nature of the hazard. / Please note that the shipper is responsible for making sure / that all the Regulations in respect of each and every / shipment are followed and so cause minimum delay at the / port. The above is an outline of the new Regulations / and the official document will be sent out as soon / as it comes to hand.

(185 words, 1.43 SI)

26

UNIT 15 *Insurance Broker*

You are working for Mavis Fry of Ivy Insurance Co.

1 LETTER TO MISS MAY BOND

New words: tour, New Zealand, coast, evening, risks

Miss May Bond, Dear Madam, Our agent has asked us / to provide you with additional insurance cover for the tour / you are making to Australia and New Zealand in October. / We understand from him that your itinerary involves one week / bookings in two towns on the Gold Coast and three / in New Zealand. We propose to issue a new policy / which will cover all your valuables for the period for / which you are out of the UK. This will / include the large number of expensive evening dresses required for / your performances. Each of these items will have to be / listed and valued separately. For this purpose we attach a / form to be completed as fully as possible and returned / direct to this office. We shall then be able to / prepare you a special policy to cover all risks and / let you know the premium required. Yours faithfully

(148 words, 1.47 SI)

2 MEMORANDUM TO ALL AGENTS

New words: relief, assurance, bonus

(To) All agents *(Heading)* TEN YEAR SAVINGS PLAN. Talks have been taking / place between a national bank and ourselves on a savings / plan that will benefit the small saver, give tax relief / and include life assurance cover. Our plan is to offer / an easy way for customers to build up capital through / small regular savings. We have an excellent record of investment / and, based on our past experience, can look forward to / making good bonus offers. A customer can save in £10 / units for a minimum period of 10 years, and / from the first payment gets automatic life assurance cover whilst / the savings plan continues in operation. In this way a / family is protected should the holder of the policy die. / The new plan is shortly to be advertised nationally and / full details will be sent to all agents within a / few days of the advertisement appearing.

(146 words, 1.52 SI)

27

3 DRAFT FOR A STANDARD LETTER
**(This will be printed with boxes against each item to be
ticked as appropriate by the sender.)**

New words: proof, renew, contents

Dear . . . Thank you for your cheque for . . . We enclose Certificate /
of Motor Insurance and official receipt. We enclose Proposal Form /
for completion and return as soon as possible with proof / of no claims
bonus. We enclose Cover Note in respect / of your vehicle. If you
wish to renew your Contents / Insurance please complete the attached
form and return it to / this office. A Schedule to attach to your Policy
is / sent herewith. Enclosed is a cheque in respect of your / recent
claim. The additional premium is . . .. Yours faithfully

(88 words, 1.50 SI)

4 NOTES TO ATTACH TO A FORM

New words: accident, dashes, notified, theft, police

(*Heading*) MOTOR ACCIDENT OR LOSS REPORT FORM. (*Sub
heading*) *Completion* Please give a / full answer to every question.
Dashes are not sufficient and / may cause delay. Please quote your
policy number on all / correspondence until a claim reference number
is notified. (*Sub heading*) *Accident* Complete / the whole of this form
with the exception of sections / 6 and 7. Remember that any correspondence received regarding the / accident must be notified or
forwarded to this Company immediately / upon receipt. You should
also tell us if any enquiry / is started. Do not try to deal with any
third / party claim yourself or make any offer of payment, or / admit
to liability. If repair work to your vehicle is / involved, obtain and
forward two estimates for the work. (*Sub Heading*) *Theft* / Complete
the whole of this form with the exception of / sections 7, 9, 10 and 12.
Settlement in respect of / theft is normally delayed until the police
have had time / to complete their enquiries. A great many vehicles are
found / within a few weeks of being reported missing. (*Sub heading*)
Fire Complete / the whole of this form with the exception of
Sections / 6, 9 and 12.

(184 words, 1.57 SI)

UNIT 16 *Department Store*

You are working for Mr R Johnson in the Accounts Section of Prince's Department Store.

1 LETTER TO MRS J GRAIN

New word: hire

Mrs J Grain, Dear Mrs Grain, (*Heading*) ACCOUNT NO. 14/5793. Thank you for sending us your / cheque for £25 against your Easy Budget Account / No. 145793. You have now / completed your monthly payments for this account, the full hire / purchase price being £200 and there is now / nothing further to pay. We shall be pleased to receive / any orders from you in the future and you may / be sure that you will always receive every attention. Yours / sincerely

(91 words, 1.35 SI)

2 STANDARD LETTER TO CUSTOMERS

New words: discourteous, efficient, bottom, remittance

Dear Sir or Madam, We hope you will not think / it discourteous of us to send you this standard letter / in reply to your enquiry but we find that this / is the most efficient way to deal quickly with customers / requirements. As you do not hold an account with us / we must ask you for complete payment in advance before / we can despatch your order. The amount is shown at / the bottom of this page. As soon as we receive / the remittance from you we will despatch your order. Yours / faithfully

(91 words, 1.35 SI)

3 LETTER TO MRS P MANNERS

New words: apologise, investigated, error, occur, instead, annoyance

Mrs P Manners, Dear Mrs Manners, I must apologise to / you for the delay in replying to your letter of / 4th January in which you said that you were overcharged / by an amount of £4 on goods which you / ordered from us last month. I have had the matter / investigated and find that an error did occur in your / account and that you were invoiced for goods amounting to / £58.90 instead of £54.90. / Therefore I am enclosing our cheque for £4 and / I would ask you to accept this with my sincere / apologies for any annoyance that this matter may have caused / you. Yours sincerely

(113 words, 1.43 SI)

4 NOTICE TO CUSTOMERS

New words: laying, carpets, queries, fitting, skirtings, furniture

(Heading) CONDITIONS ON THE PURCHASE AND LAYING OF ALL CARPETS. 1. / A deposit has to be paid on all goods or / they will only be held in stock for up to / 14 days from the date of the estimate. 2. If there / are any queries about fitting they should be raised prior / to the acceptance of the estimate. We regret that changes / cannot be made after carpets have been cut and fitted. / 3. Please make sure that all self-laid carpets are / checked for design, size and quality before cutting takes place. / No changes can be made after the carpets have been / cut and laid. 4. It is not possible to accept / responsibility for any damage that may occur accidentally to electric, / gas or water services which run under the floors or / around the skirtings of your house. 5. The customer must / move all furniture and existing carpets and make sure that / doors are eased should this be required. 6. Customers must / agree to pay the carpet fitter any balance of money / due once he has completed the job. In the case / of self-laid carpets customers must pay the car-man / upon delivery.

(192 words, 1.44 SI)

UNIT 17 *Residents' Association*

You are assisting the Secretary of the North Reach Residents' Association.

1 CIRCULAR LETTER TO ALL MEMBERS

New words: doubling, guardians, residents, retiring, sparing, join

Dear Member, *(Heading)* HELP WANTED. We are very pleased to tell / you that we have now over 4500 / Members of the Association and it is only a shortage / of help that is stopping us from doubling

30

that figure. / We have acted as guardians of residents' rights for nearly / fifty years with a fair degree of success. At the / moment on the committee we are six members short and / in addition five members are over retiring age. So will / you please consider sparing us a portion of your time / and join our committee? You would be asked to serve / on one sub-committee which meets once a month to / prepare matters to be brought to the main meeting which / is held every third Tuesday. If you feel you would / like to help please phone me right away and we / can talk about it. Yours sincerely, Secretary

(147 words, 1.37 SI)

2 NEWS SHEET

New words: transport, entrance, efforts, vandals, Bridge, social

(Main heading) NEWS SHEET No. 159. Secretary's report to Members / of the North Reach Residents' Association. As usual my report / covers items of work and problems which have been dealt / with by your Committee over the last three months. I / have grouped the items under the headings of our various / sub-committees. *(Shoulder heading)* TRANSPORT *(Paragraph heading)* *North Reach Station Pay Telephone* Over a / long period of time your Committee has tried to get / a public phone put into the station entrance hall. You / will recall that at the AGM I reported / on our efforts to bring this matter to a successful / end but it is now clear that no progress has / been made and that a telephone will not be installed / after all. The two main reasons given are that it / would not be profitable and that it would not be / possible to stop vandals damaging it at night. *(Paragraph heading)* *New Train / Time-Tables* A meeting has been arranged with the General / Manager at London Bridge station in order to exchange views / on the proposed new train time-tables from North Reach / to London. *(Shoulder heading)* SOCIAL SERVICES We have formed a new Sub- / Committee to put forward the Association's views in this important / area of work. A meeting was held with the Health / Authority when the main discussion was on possible Health Service / cuts and the effect that this would have on North / Reach Hospital. Members will have read the results of this / in the local papers. *(Shoulder heading)* PARKS AND HIGHWAYS We are pleased / to note that, following pressure from us, it has been / decided to plant flower beds on the east side of / the common thus improving considerably the view from the main / road. Finally please note that the AGM will / be held on Friday, 6th April and not on Thursday, / 29th March as stated in the last News Sheet. /

(310 words, 1.39 SI)

3 LETTER TO MR S PAGE

New words: invite, neighbour, crime, prevention

Mr S Page, Dear Mr Page, Your name was given / to our Chairman by Mr and Mrs Day who suggested / that we should write to you to invite you to / become a member of our Association. We understand from them / that you have only recently come to live in North / Reach and that you are a near neighbour of the / Days. We also believe that you have served for a / number of years in the Police Force and could advise / us on crime prevention in our area. We should be / very glad to welcome you into our Association and look / forward to hearing from you. Yours sincerely

(107 words, 1.38 SI)

UNIT 18 *Bank Area Office*

You are secretary to the Manager, Mr Peter England.

1 LETTER TO MR R SWEET

New words: overdraft, debit, comply

Mr R Sweet, Dear Sir, Further to our letter dated / 20th May setting out our agreement with you that your / overdraft limit of £500 would be reduced by / £100 each month with effect from 1st June, / I have to point out that the overdraft should by / now have reduced to £300 but it is / in fact £600 debit, an excess of / £300. This position is not acceptable and I would / ask you to let me have an immediate remittance so / that your current acount is once again maintained within the / agreed level of overdraft. If you are not able to / comply with this request I should appreciate your comments as / to whether you expect any further delay in receiving sufficient / funds. In any case I expect you will make a / transfer from your deposit account immediately. I hope to hear / from you by return regarding these two points. Yours faithfully /

(160 words, 1.45 SI)

2 LETTER TO MR DAVID LONG

New words: David, Gravely, scheme, promised, joint

Mr David Long, Dear David, *(Heading)* GRAVELY DEVELOP-MENT. I thank you / and Mr Rule for coming to see me last week /

about this provincial development scheme. As promised I have read / through all the documents you left with me. However, I / regret to have to advise you that our Head Office / feels that it is unable to meet your request for / a development loan of two million pounds. As I told / you at our meeting the maximum finance we could consider / providing would be 50% of land costs and / two-thirds of building costs. Your balance represents 100% / of building costs plus finance charges and fees. / We think it might enable the Gravely Development to proceed / if you entered into a joint development agreement with the / building group you mentioned to me at our meeting. I / am very sorry to be unable to help in this / matter but in the circumstances I am sure you understand / the Bank's position. Do keep in touch with me. Kind / regards, Yours sincerely

(173 words, 1.46 SI)

3   LETTER TO MR AND MRS R BOOKER

New words: unemployment, sickness

Mr and Mrs R Booker, Dear Mr and Mrs Booker, / (*Heading*) BUDGET ACCOUNT RENEWAL I see from my records that the / final payment on this year's Budget Account will be made / in two weeks' time on 1st March. I hope you / have found this service useful and that you will decide / to continue for a further twelve months so I am / writing to draw your attention to an important change to / the scheme which is now available. A Budget Protection Plan / has been started covering unemployment, sickness and accident. The premium / would be charged monthly to your current account. I enclose / full details for you to study. Yours sincerely

(108 words, 1.45 SI)

4   LETTER TO MR R PRICE, COMPANY SECRETARY, GOLD & MASTERS LTD

New words: Waverley, relationship, plots, solicitors, sworn

Dear Mr Price, With regard to your scheme for raising / capital for the new housing programme at Waverley and the / question of a suitable security, I have now heard from / my Head Office that because of our long standing business / relationship over the years they are agreeable to taking a / second charge on the three plots of land owned by / House-Building Limited. An outline of the legal steps to / be taken is that it will be necessary for House- / Building Limited to transfer the properties into your name as / owner. Then the Bank's solicitors will present a draft mortgage / and submit it to your solicitors. When this draft is / agreed it will be sent for registration to Companies House. / When the loan has been repaid a sworn statement to / this effect will be sent to the Registrar at Companies / House to be recorded in your file there. My Head / Office have also agreed that the maximum period of time / for you to have this loan will be six years / from the date of registration and that the rate of / interest to be charged will be one per cent above / current base rate. I look forward to having your written / agreement to these conditions and I will then put the / work in hand with the Bank's solicitors. Yours sincerely

(219 words, 1.43 SI)

5 MEMORANDUM TO BILL WARR, COMPANY SECRETARY

New words: **canteen, subsidy, offset, disposal, decorating, block**

(*To*) Bill Warr (*Heading*) STAFF ASSOCIATION. As you know I leave shortly / for a three month tour of Australia. Among the outstanding / matters is the report I made after attending the last / SA committee meeting. My job on that committee is / to represent management and the report I made can now / be put to the next Board of Directors meeting by / you on the basis of an exchange of views between / myself and the Chairman of the SA. He voiced / his concern that management has not yet taken action on / some canteen items. From our discussion it is clear that / the degree to which we can approve the remaining canteen / items will influence staff relations for the better. To keep / the amount spent within the budget my recommendations are: 1. / An evening meals service for staff who happen to stay / late. 2. A subsidy on meals to offset the rise / in price across meat, bread and milk. 3. A new / waste disposal unit. 4. Decorating canteen—clean off, fill in / holes and paint walls. From my memory of the estimate / it was about £800. I was surprised to / learn in my talk with the SA Chairman that / out of next year's budget he wants an assurance that / the Directors will commit themselves to building a new gentlemen's / toilet block. The Board and SA do not appear / to differ on priorities for the canteen so whatever is / agreed is sure to have the approval of the S/A. Sorry we shall not meet before I leave on / Monday.

(261 words, 1.42 SI)

34

UNIT 19 *Stationers*

You are working for the Administration Manager of Stationery Sales Ltd.

1 LETTER TO MESSRS W R WORTH & SONS

New words: Messrs, Sons, stationery, unforeseen

For the attention of Mr J J Fish (*To*) Messrs W / R Worth & Sons, Dear Sirs, (*Heading*) NEW CONTRACT PRICES. With / reference to your recent discussions with our Area Sales Manager, / Mr Trueman, we now have much pleasure in sending you / our cheapest stationery contract prices. You will notice that all / the prices quoted on the enclosed list do not include / VAT and are subject to a monthly discount / of 2½%. As usual, carriage / is free on deliveries of £50 and upwards. We / expect to be able to hold these prices until early / next year, subject to any unforeseen or unusual cost increases, / in which case we should let you know immediately. Yours / faithfully

(121 words, 1.46 SI)

2 LETTER TO SALES MANAGER, LINES TYPEWRITER ACCESSORIES LTD

New words: Typewriter, Accessories, faulty, dozen, ribbons

Sales Manager, Lines Typewriter Accessories Ltd, Dear Sir, (*Heading*) FAULTY RIBBONS / We enclose a copy of a letter we have received / this morning from our customers Messrs Loveless Brothers. You will / see from this letter that they have returned two dozen / faulty typewriter ribbons which were supplied by ourselves about a / month ago and purchased from your Company. We are enclosing / one of the ribbons in question and we should be / most grateful if you would look into this complaint without / delay and let us have your comments. Messrs Loveless Brothers / have been very good customers of ours for a number / of years and we should like to be able to / reply to their complaint as soon as possible. Yours faithfully /

(120 words, 1.49 SI)

3 LETTER TO G R MARKS & COMPANY, INSURANCE BROKERS

New words: Brokers, authority

G R Marks & Company, Insurance Brokers, Dear Sirs, (*Heading*) POLICY / NO XCB6787. We enclose / a completed claim form in

35

respect of an accident involving / one of our sales representatives, Mr Short. He was driving / one of our Company's cars, registration No. A15/7PDQ. This car is insured with your / Company under the above policy. It will be necessary for / us to rent a replacement vehicle until all repairs have / been completed. We should be glad to have your authority / to go ahead and obtain a similar make of car / as soon as possible. I should like to speak to / you about this matter so perhaps you would be kind / enough to phone me when you receive this letter so / that we can make immediate arrangements with the rental company. / Yours faithfully

(142 words, 1.49 SI)

4 LETTER TO QUICK-WORK PRINTERS LTD

New words: Printers, compliments, slips, congratulate, style

Quick-Work Printers Ltd, Dear Sirs, We wish to thank / you very much for sending us so quickly the proofs / of our new letter-headings and compliments slips. We should / like to congratulate you on the excellent style and layout / of this work. We are now enclosing our Order No. / LX7784 and we would ask / you to make quite sure that the correct weight of / paper is used ie 100 gsm. / Perhaps you will advise us as to the earliest possible / delivery date as our stocks are running very low. We / are also thinking of having some of our standard forms / and analysis sheets redesigned in a different style. We should / be grateful if you would ask your representative to call / on us the next time he is in this area / so that we can discuss our requirements in some detail. / Yours faithfully

(152 words, 1.37 SI)

UNIT 20 *Audio-Visual Aids*

You are working for the Marketing Manager of Audio-Visual Aids PLC.

1 LETTER TO MR B CRYER

New words: tapes, audio, visual, packages, delegation, popular

Mr B Cryer, Dear Sir, Thank you very much for / your enquiry dated 21st April regarding our programmes for / in-company training. We note that you are quoting from / an out-of-date brochure so we are sending you / a copy of our latest catalogue. This gives a full / list of all our current books and tapes and quotes / standard prices as well as special offers of complete audio / visual packages. As requested we are sending you a selection / of our 'Notes for Staff' booklets including 'Job Analysis', 'What / to Look For When Interviewing', 'The Writing of Reports', 'Dealing / with the Public' and 'Delegation of Duties'. The answer to / your question on the subject of meetings is yes, we / have two excellent books, one written to assist the chairman / and the other is of particular interest to the minuting / secretary. These books are very popular and I am sorry / to say that neither is in stock at the moment. / I will send you a copy of both the books / as soon as they are reprinted. Yours faithfully

(178 words, 1.47 SI)

2 LETTER TO MR C STRANGE

New words: series, video, studio, college

Mr C Strange, Dear Mr Strange, My secretary has just / given me your telephone message. She says that you would / like to come to our offices as soon as possible / in order to view our two recent series of video / programmes, one on computers and the other on word processing. / We are presenting these in our television studio next Tuesday, / 26th April, for the benefit of a group of / students from a local college. You would be most welcome / if you would like to join the party. We shall / be starting at 10 am. Perhaps you would care / to have lunch with me afterwards? Yours sincerely

(108 words, 1.44 SI)

3 LETTER TO MESSRS STOREY & WATCHAM

New words: aspects, chalk, lectures, avoid

For the attention of Mr F Brake. (*To*) Messrs Storey & / Watcham, Dear Sirs, I understand from one of our salesmen / that your firm has expressed considerable interest in the courses / which we run on all aspects of communication in business. / These courses are far from being 'talk and chalk' lectures / and they include films, role playing, discussions and case histories. / We take only a dozen people at one time so that / there is a great deal of personal attention. There is / so much demand at the moment that we have built / up a short waiting list of firms who would like / to take part. The earliest time we could accommodate your / staff is at the end of May or early in / June. In the meanwhile I am sending you full details / and would ask you to apply as soon as possible / to avoid any further delay. Yours faithfully

(147 words, 1.41 SI)

4 LETTER TO MRS E YARDLEY

New words: edition, either, Italian, Spanish

Mrs E Yardley, Dear Mrs Yardley, Thank you for your / letter of 24th April which was addressed to Mr / Massey who is no longer working for us. I have / taken his place as Marketing Manager. I see from our / records that you have been a customer of ours for / several years and that you regularly receive our advertising material. / Details of our recent books and video tapes will be / in the post to you today. You will notice that / we have a new edition of our booklet on Health / and Safety Regulations and another on Security. I think that / your students would find both of these very useful and I / enclose a complimentary copy. In answer to your question regarding / language books and tapes I am sorry that we do / not have any in either Italian or Spanish. Please let / me know if there is anything else that you need. / Yours sincerely

(152 words, 1.48 SI)

Key

UNIT 1

1.

New words: meter ⁓⁓⁓   Yours faithfully ⁓⁓

(shorthand outline passage)

2.

New words: select ⁓⁓   vouchers ⁓⁓   stamps ⁓⁓

stick ⁓⁓

(shorthand outline passage)

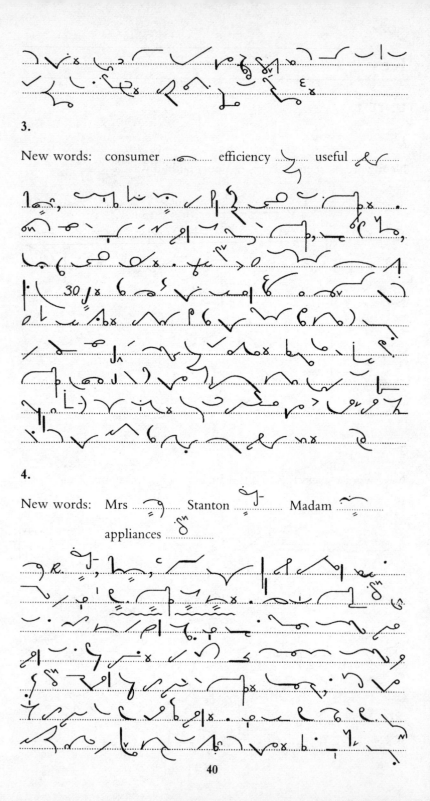

3.

New words: consumer   ......   efficiency   ......   useful   ......

4.

New words: Mrs   ......   Stanton   ......   Madam   ......

appliances   ......

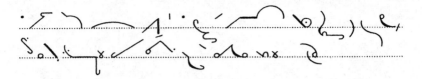

UNIT 2

1.

New words: Dennis 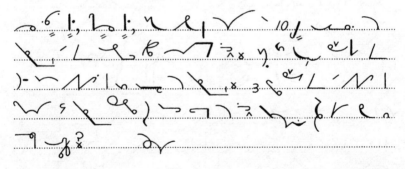 James central

2.

New words: Sally _____ Yours sincerely _____

3.

New words: agency _____ lunch _____ withdrawals _____

enquiries _____ efficiently _____

parking _____

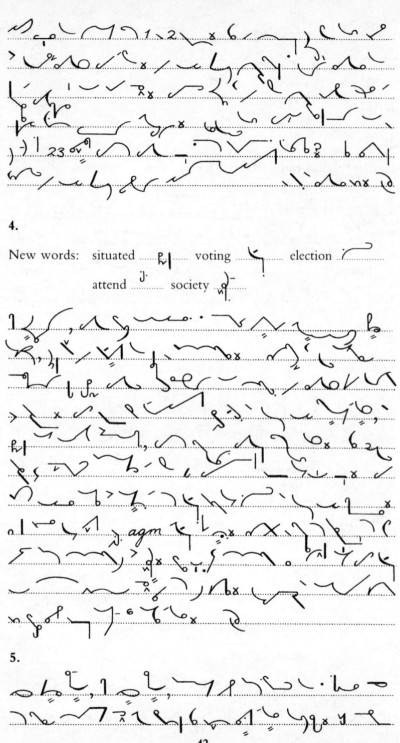

4.

New words: situated   voting   election   attend   society

5.

42

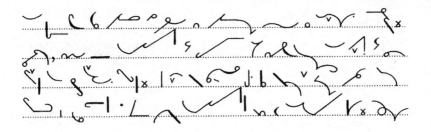

UNIT 3

1.

New words: bulbs ....⁀⌣... satisfaction ...ƒ... bonemeal ...×...⁚...

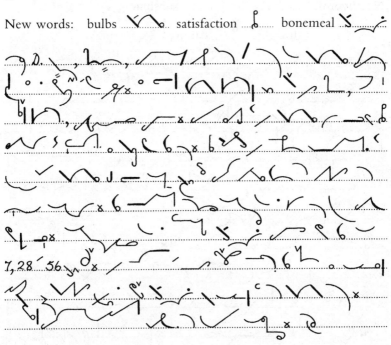

2.

New words: improvements ...⌢⌣... garden ...⟋... flower ...⌡...

paths ...⟍... measurements ...⟋...

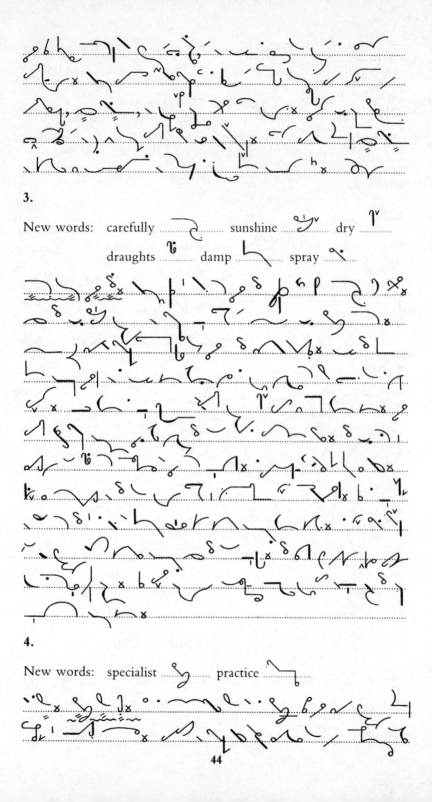

3.

New words: carefully _____ sunshine _____ dry _____

draughts _____ damp _____ spray _____

4.

New words: specialist _____ practice _____

44

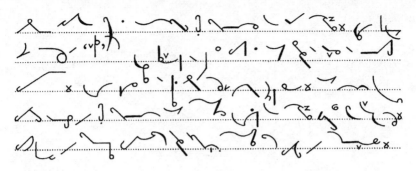

UNIT 4

1.

New words: expensive ⌇⌇⌇⌇⌇ dining-room ⌇⌇⌇⌇⌇ bars ⌇⌇⌇⌇⌇

Motel ⌇⌇⌇⌇⌇

2.

New words: advertisement ⌇⌇⌇⌇⌇ automatically ⌇⌇⌇⌇⌇

enter ⌇⌇⌇⌇⌇ computer ⌇⌇⌇⌇⌇

economical ⌇⌇⌇⌇⌇ modernised ⌇⌇⌇⌇⌇

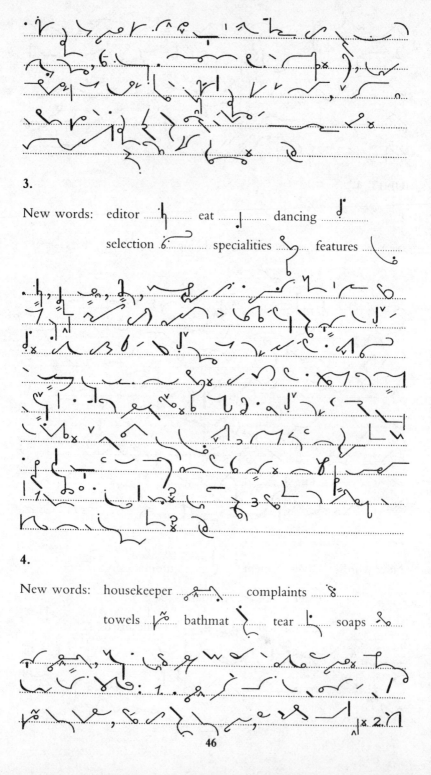

3.

New words: editor   eat   dancing

selection   specialities   features

4.

New words: housekeeper   complaints

towels   bathmat   tear   soaps

46

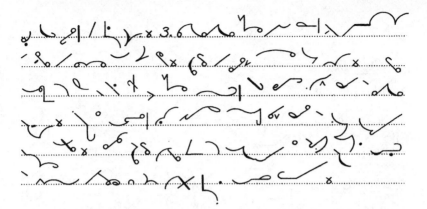

UNIT 5

1.

New words: Walter .... Pan .... profitable ....

London ....

2.

New words: aunt .... Jane .... divided ....

Sydney .... Australia .... vacant ....

47

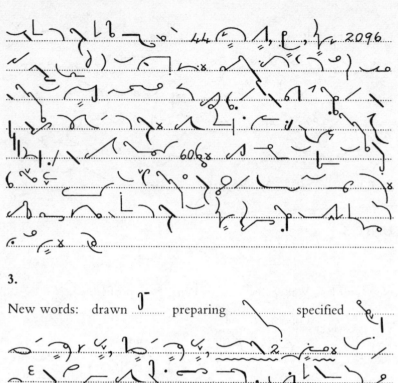

3.

New words: drawn ⌡⁻   preparing ⟋   specified ⟍

4.

New words: officer ⟋   extension ⊤   already ⋀

objection ⟍   surveyor ⌁

48

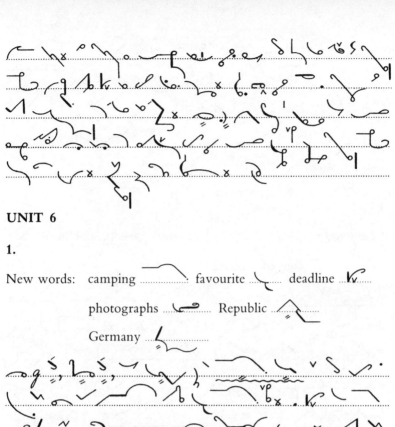

UNIT 6

1.

New words: camping ⌒ : favourite ⌟ deadline ⌐

photographs ⌣ Republic ⌃

Germany ⌟

2.

New words: holiday ⌐ . circle ⌀ entry ⌐

prize ⌐ Amsterdam ⌐ Paris ⌄

A   B

49

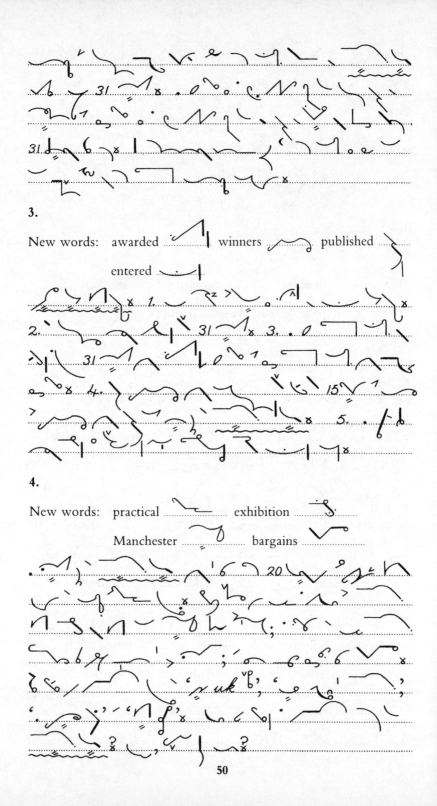

3.

New words: awarded   winners   published   entered

4.

New words: practical   exhibition   Manchester   bargains

5.

New words: abroad 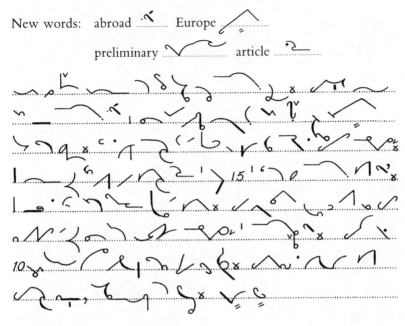 Europe

preliminary .... article ....

UNIT 7

1.

2.

New words: Harry .... Secretary ....

51

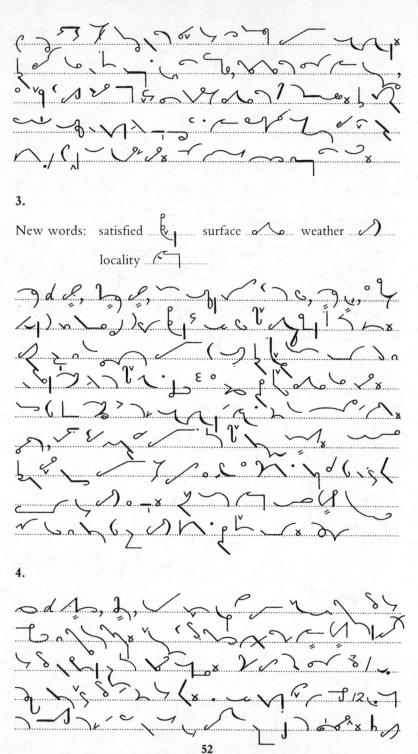

3.

New words: satisfied ⎇ surface ⌣ weather ⟋ locality ⌐

4.

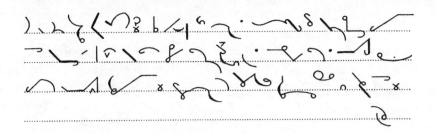

UNIT 8

1.

New words: private ⟍ admitted ⌐

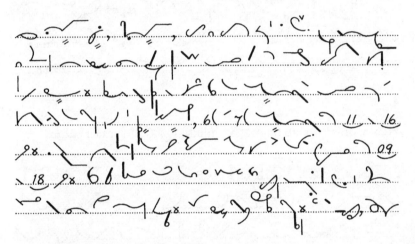

2.

New words: badges ⟩ communication ⌐⟍

visitors ⟍ wears ⌐⟍ security ⌐

3.

New words: desks ⌐⌐ telex ⌐⌐ halls ⌐⌐ exit ⌐⌐

(shorthand outlines) 24 28

24(25(09 18

26(09 16

(shorthand outlines)

99; a, 0 1 199; b,

2 299 b, 0 3 399

4.

New words: exhibiting ⌐⌐ films ⌐⌐ exact ⌐⌐

(shorthand outlines) 3

(shorthand outlines)

UNIT 9

1.

New words: Pamela ⌐⌐ specimen ⌐⌐

manuscript ⌐⌐ despatch ⌐⌐

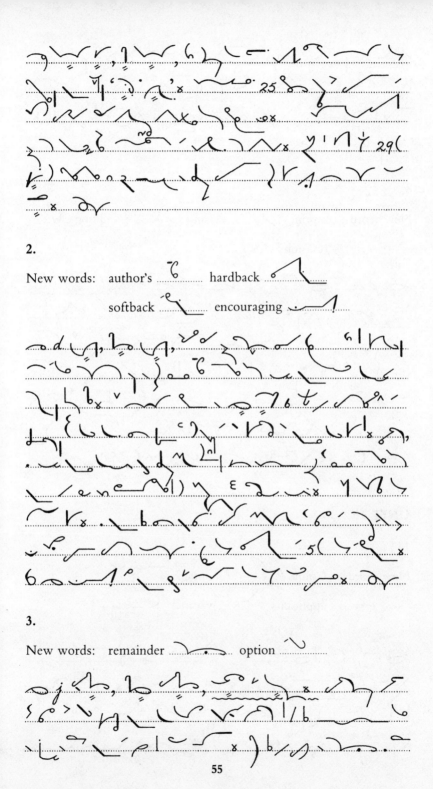

2.

New words: author's ⸜ hardback ⸜⸝

softback ⸜⸝ encouraging ⸜⸝

3.

New words: remainder ⸜⸝ option ⸜⸝

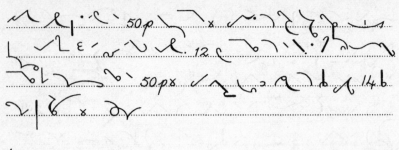

4.

New words: reprint 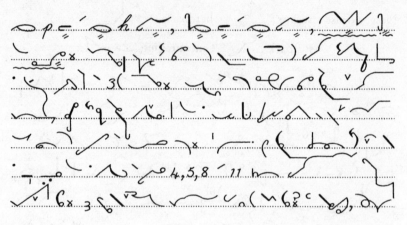 revising _____ edition _____

revision _____

UNIT 10

1.

New words: Colin _____ accountant _____

applicants _____ vacancy _____

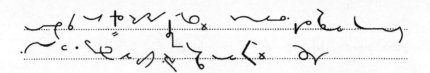

2.

New words: departmental ⟨shorthand⟩   necessarily ⟨shorthand⟩

   attendance ⟨shorthand⟩

(shorthand passage)

3.

(shorthand passage)

57

4.

New words: Journal ⟋⟍ alone ⟋ holder ⟍

(shorthand outline passage)

UNIT 11

1.

New words: postmaster ⟍ envelope ⟍⟍

eventually ⟍ destination ⟍

tickets ⟍ contained ⟍

(shorthand outline passage)

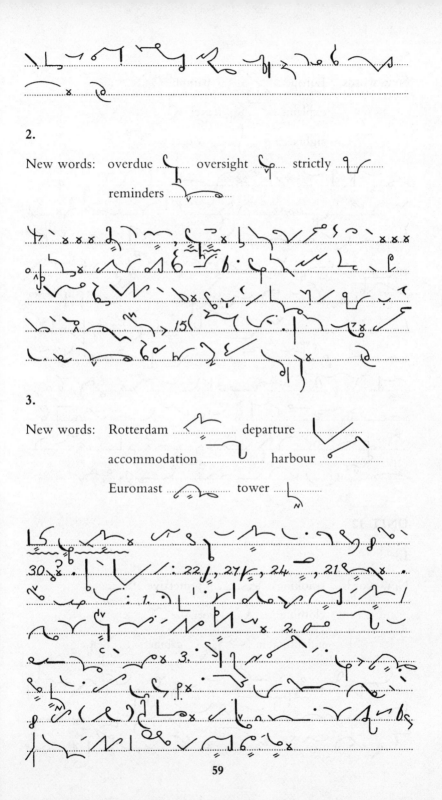

2.

New words: overdue _____ oversight _____ strictly _____

reminders _____

3.

New words: Rotterdam _____ departure _____

accommodation _____ harbour _____

Euromast _____ tower _____

59

4.

New words: Europe ⌃ pamphlet ⌢

explains ⌐ travel ⌡

sightseeing ⌡ Moscow ⌐

(shorthand outlines)

UNIT 12

1.

New words: smoking ⌐ protective ⌐

clothing ⌐ worn ⌐

inflammable ⌐ cabinets ⌐

(shorthand outlines)

60

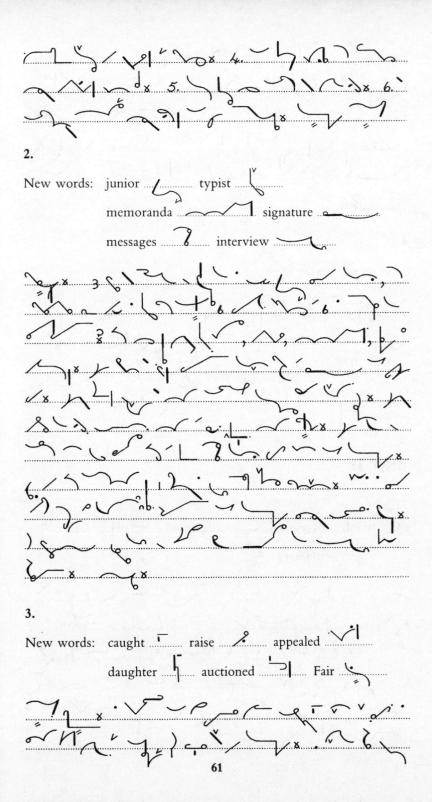

2.

New words: junior ⟋⟍ typist ⟍

memoranda ⟍⟍⟍ signature ⟋⟍

messages ⟍ interview ⟍⟍

3.

New words: caught ⟋ raise ⟋ appealed ⟍

daughter ⟍ auctioned ⟍ Fair ⟍

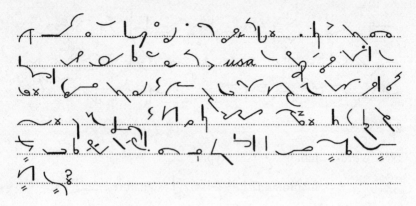

4.

New word: Paul ⌣

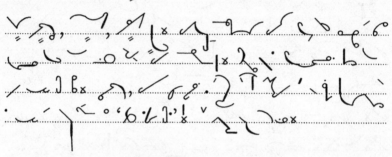

UNIT 13

1.

New words: overseas ⌐ organised ⌐ draft ℧

itinerary ⌐

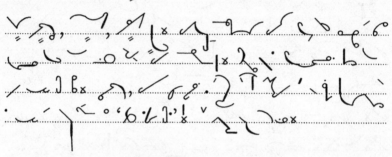

62

2.

New words: Chairman 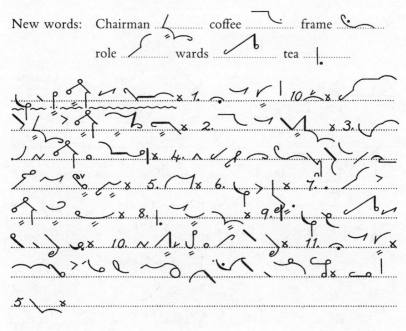 coffee _____ frame _____

role _____ wards _____ tea _____

3.

New words: Terry _____ Wood _____ ˙intensive _____

aids _____

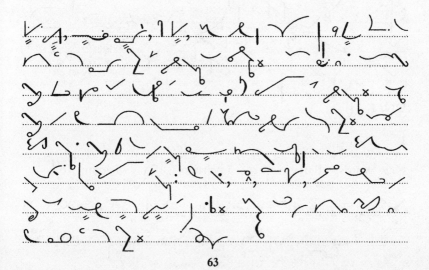

63

4.

New words: waiting  treatment  stay 

toilet  admission 

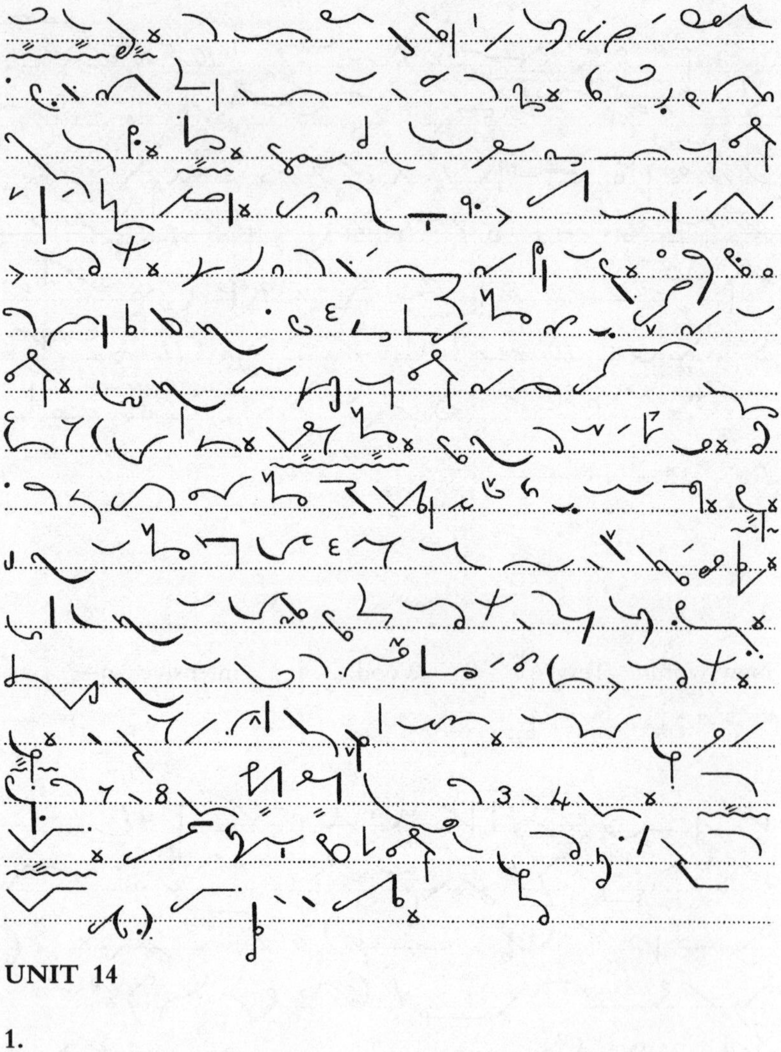

UNIT 14

1.

New words: Barry  Liverpool 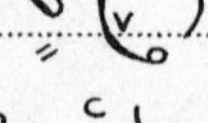 Lading 

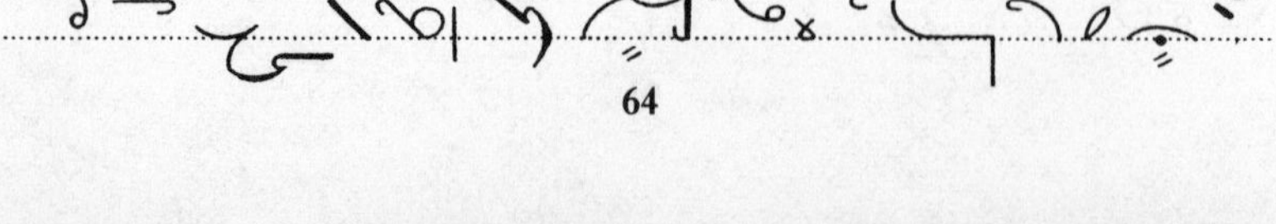

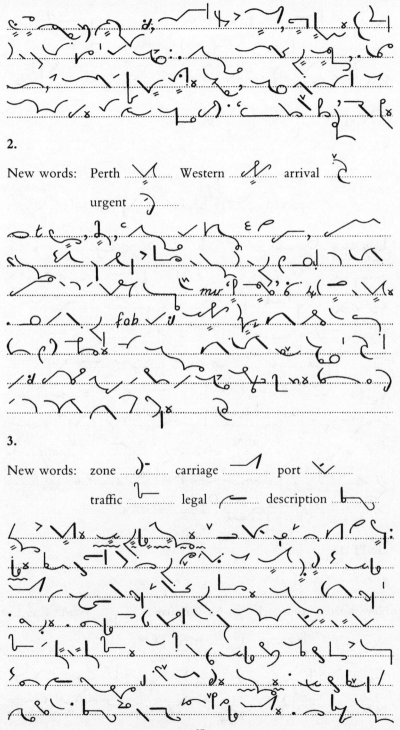

2.

New words: Perth ⟍⟋ Western ⟋ arrival ⌇

urgent ⟩

3.

New words: zone ⟩– carriage ⟋ port ⌄

traffic ⌐ legal ⟋ description ⌐

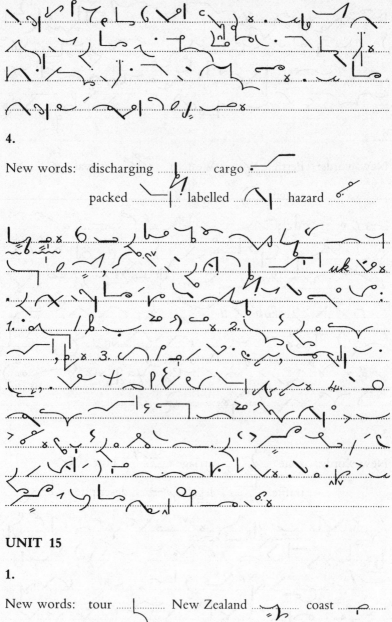

4.

New words: discharging .... cargo ....

packed .... labelled .... hazard ....

UNIT 15

1.

New words: tour .... New Zealand .... coast ....

evening .... risks ....

66

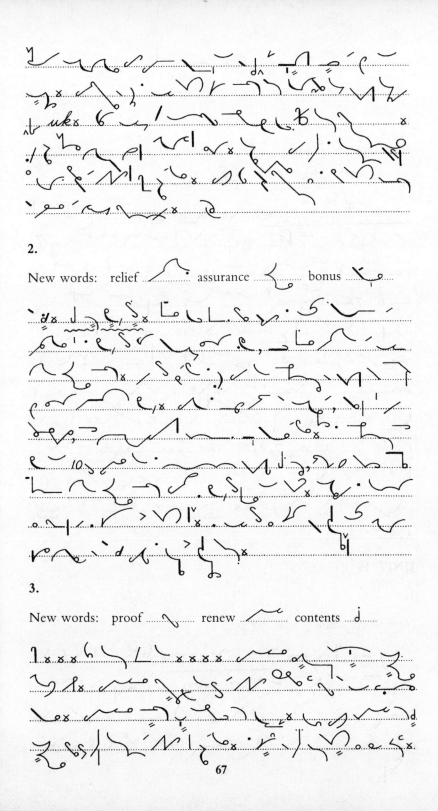

2.

New words: relief ⌇⌇⌇ assurance ⌇⌇⌇ bonus ⌇⌇⌇

3.

New words: proof ⌇⌇⌇ renew ⌇⌇⌇ contents ⌇⌇⌇

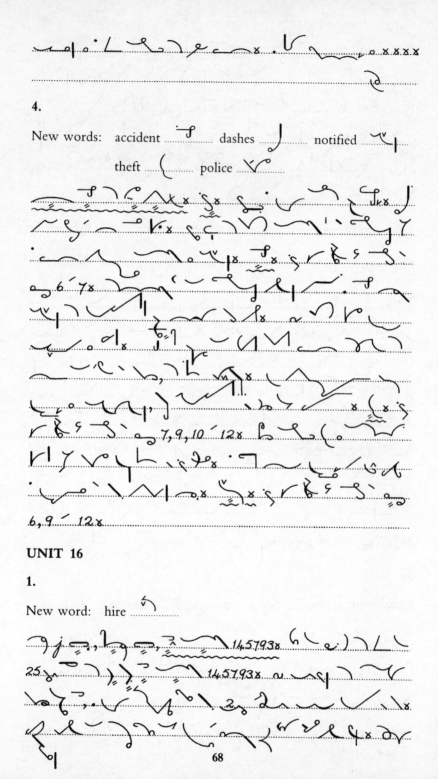

4.

New words: accident _____ dashes _____ notified _____

theft _____ police _____

UNIT 16

1.

New word: hire _____

2.

New words: discourteous .... efficient ....

bottom .... remittance ....

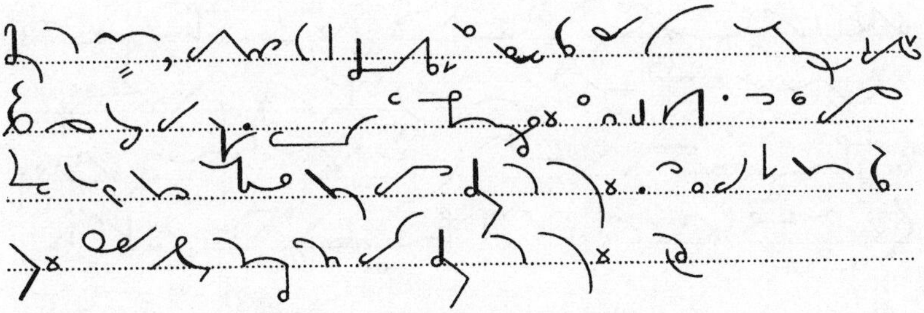

3.

New words: apologise .... investigated ....

error .... occur .... instead ....

annoyance ....

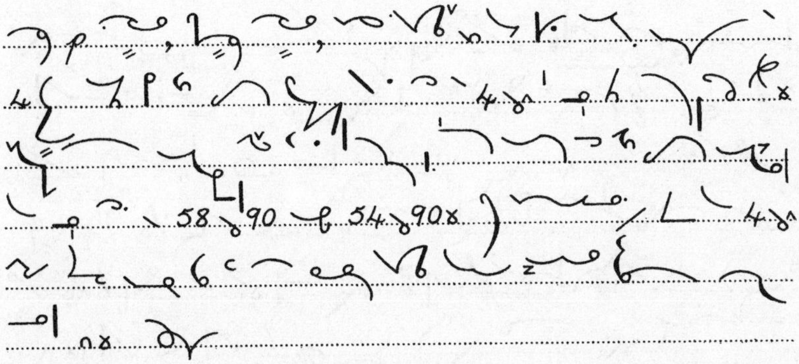

4.

New words: laying .... carpets .... queries ....

fitting .... skirtings .... furniture ....

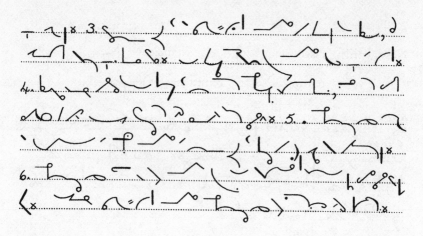

UNIT 17

1.

New words: doubling ____ guardians ____ residents ____

retiring ____ sparing ____ join ____

2.

New words: transport ____ entrance ____ efforts ____

vandals ____ Bridge ____ social ____

159

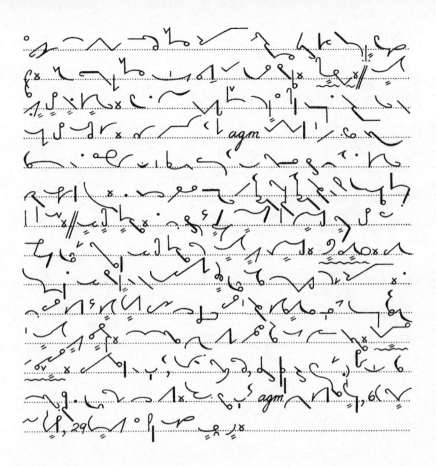

3.

New words: invite ‿ᴠ neighbour ‿ᴀ crime ᵛ

prevention ‿ᴌ

UNIT 18

1.

New words: overdraft .... debit .... comply ....

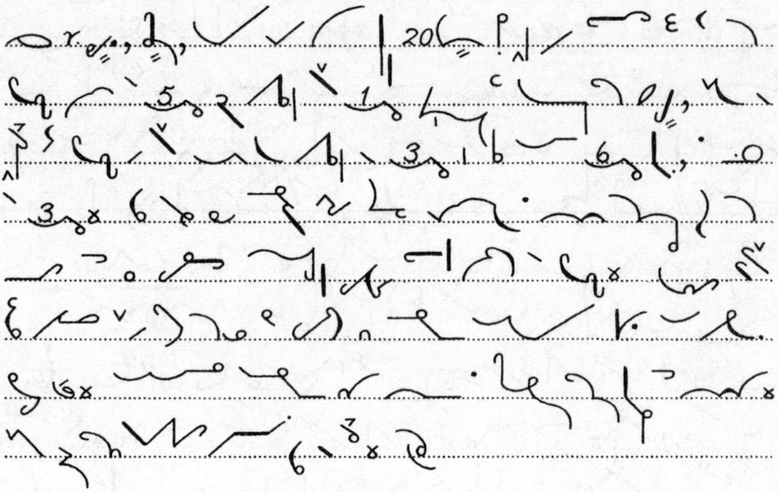

2.

New words: David .... Gravely .... scheme ....

promised .... joint ....

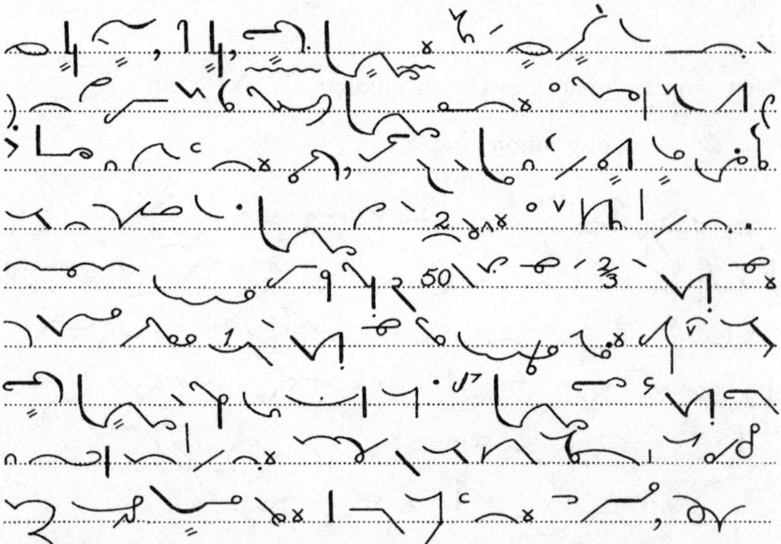

3.

New words: unemployment 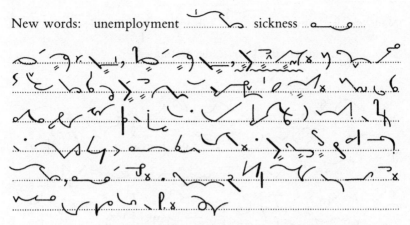 sickness

4.

New words: Waverley .... relationship ....

plots .... solicitors .... sworn ....

5.

New words: canteen ⌐⌐   subsidy ⌐°   offset ⌐°

disposal ⌐⌐   decorating ⌐⌐.

block ⌐⌐

[shorthand outlines]

UNIT 19

1.

New words: Messrs ⌐⌐   Sons ⌐⌐   stationery ⌐⌐

unforeseen ⌐⌐

[shorthand outlines]

74

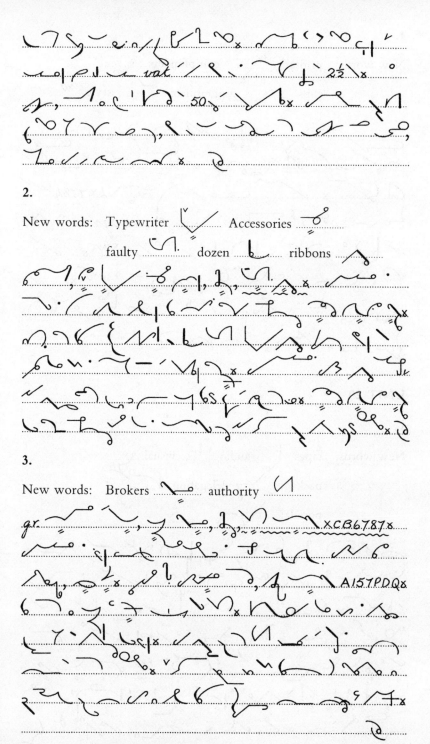

2.

New words: Typewriter _____ Accessories _____

faulty _____ dozen _____ ribbons _____

3.

New words: Brokers _____ authority _____

XCB6787x

A157PDQx

4.

New words: printers .... compliments ....
slips .... congratulate .... style ....

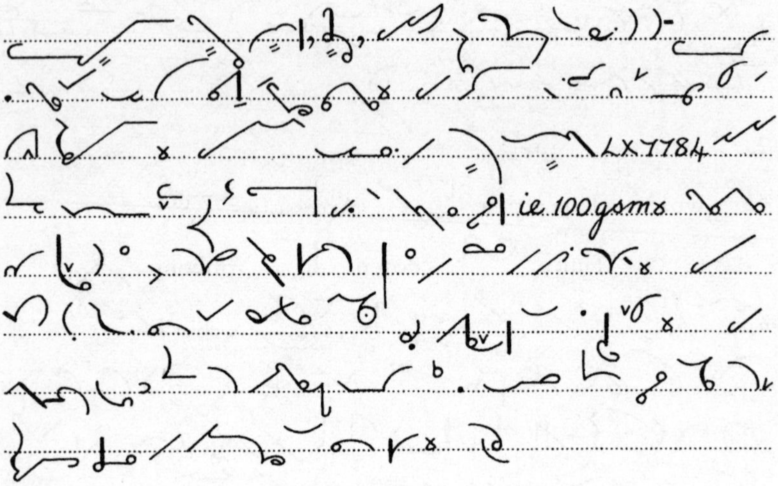
LX7784
ie 100gsm

UNIT 20

1.

New words: tapes .... audio .... visual ....
packages .... delegation ....
popular ....

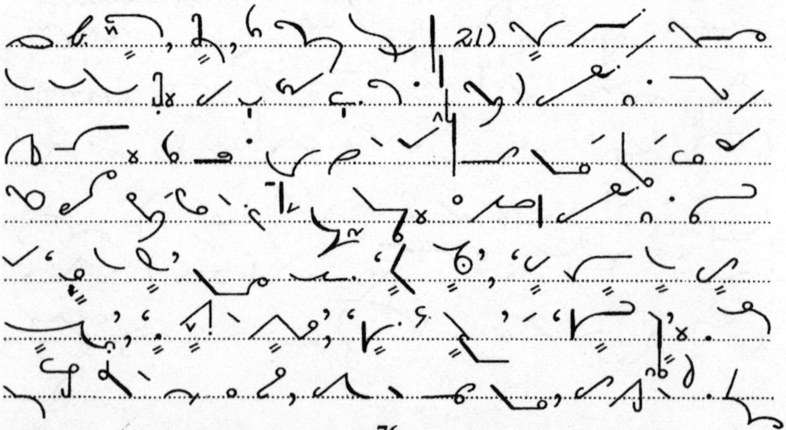
21)

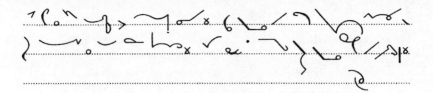

2.

New words: series ⌇ video ⌇ studio ⌇

college ⌇

3.

New words: aspects ⌇ chalk ⌇ lectures ⌇

avoid ⌇

4.

New words: edition 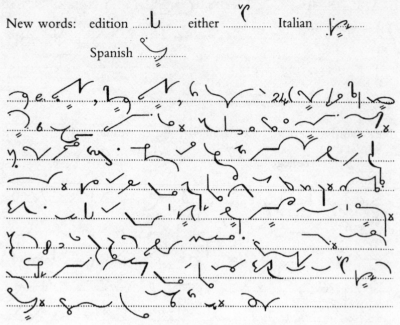 either Italian

Spanish

List of Outlines

a		advertising	
able		advice	
about		advise	
above		advised	
accept		advising	
accordance		*after*	
according		*again*	
accordingly		against	
account		age	
accounts		agent	
acknowledge		*ago*	
act		*agree*	
action		agreed	
actual		agreement	
actually		*air*	
add		*all*	
addition		allow	
additional		allowance	
address		allowed	
addressed		*along*	
advance		already	
advantage		*also*	

although		approved	
always		approximately	
am		*are*	
amount		area	
amounts		areas	
an		around	
analysis		arrange	
and		arranged	
annual		arrangement	
another		arrangements	
answer		arrived	
any		*as*	
anything		*ask*	
apparently		asked	
appear		assist	
appears		assistance	
applicable		association	
application		assure	
applied		*at*	
apply		attached	
appraisal		*attention*	
appreciate		automatic	
appreciated		available	
approval		average	

80

aware		be	
		because	
across		become	
advertise		been	
afternoon		before	
altogether★		behalf	
among		being	
animal		believe	
announce		below	
April		benefit	
arm★		benefits	
art		best	
attempt		better	
August		between	
authority		bill	
away		board	
		bond	
		bonds	
back		book	
balance		both	
bank		branch	
based		bring	
basic		brochure	
basis		brought	

81

budget		brother	
building		build	
business		built	
but		burn	
by		buy/bye	

baby★			
bad★			
base		call	
beautiful		called	
bed		can	
begin		cannot	
behind		capacity	
belief		capital	
beyond★		car	
big		card	
black		cards	
blue		carried	
body★		carry	
bought		cars	
boy/buoy		case	
brake		cases	
bread		cash	
break		catalogue	

cause		come	
centre		coming	
certain		comments	
certainly		committee	
certificate		*common*	
certificates		companies	
change		*company*	
changed		company's	
changes		*complete*	
charge		completed	
charged		completely	
charges		completion	
check		concerned	
checked		concerning	
checking		concrete	
cheque		*condition*	
cheques		conditions	
circumstances		confirm	
city		confirmation	
claim		connection	
claims		*consider*	
class		considerable	
clear		consideration	
close		considered	

construction		customs	
contact		cut	
continue			
contract		came	
control		care	
convenience		cell	
conversation		character★	
co-operation		cheap	
copies		chief	
copy		child	
correct		children	
correspondence		clean	
cost		coal	
costs		coarse★	
could		cold	
course		colour	
cover		comfort	
coverage		commit	
covered		competition	
covering		connect	
credit		country	
current		cry	
customer		custom	
customers			

damage		difficult	
data		direct	
date		directly	
dated		directors	
day		discount	
days		discuss	
deal		discussed	
dealers		discussion	
decide		distribution	
decided		district	
decision		division	
delay		do	
delivered		documents	
delivery		does	
demand		doing	
department		dollars	
deposit		done	
design		door	
details		doubt	
determine		down	
development		drawings	
did		due	
difference		duplicate	
different		during	

85

duty		earlier	
		earliest	
danger		early	
dear		earnings	
December		effect	
deep★		effective	
degree		either	
deliver		employee	
depend		employees	
desire★		enclose	
detail		enclosed	
develop		enclosing	
die/dye		end	
differ		engineering	
difficulty		enough	
discover		entire	
distance		equipment	
distribute		error	
dress		established	
drink		estate	
drive		estimate	
		estimated	
		etc	
		even	
each			

event		*employ*	
every		*engine★*	
example		*engineer*	
excellent		*English*	
excess		*equal*	
exchange		*ever*	
existing		*except*	
expect		*exist*	
expected		*expert*	
expense		*eye/ay*	
experience			
experienced			
express		facilities	
extend		*fact*	
extended		factory	
extra		*fall*	
extremely		*far*	
		federal	
earth★		fee	
ease		*feel*	
east		feet, ft	
education		felt	
electric		*few*	
electricity		*field*	

87

figure		free	
figures		freight	
file		from	
fill		full	
final		fully	
financial		fund	
find		funds	
fire		further	
firm		future	
first			
five			
floor		face	
f.o.b.		family	
follow		farm	
following		father	
follows		fear★	
foot		February	
for		fish	
form		fly	
forms		food	
forward		force	
forwarded		frequent	
found		Friday	
four		friend	

88

front		guarantee	
		gave	
gas		*gentlemen*	
general		*girl*	
generally		*gold*	
get		*govern*	
getting		*ground*	
give		*grow*	
given			
giving			
glad		*had*	
glass		*half*	
go		*hand*	
going		handled	
good		handling	
goods		*happy*	
government		*has*	
grain		*have*	
grade		*having*	
great		*he*	
greatly		head	
group		hear	
growth		hearing	

heating		happen	
heavy		hard	
held		health	
help		heart	
helpful		heat	
her		heir*	
here		himself	
herewith		history	
hesitate		hole	
high		horse	
higher			
him			
his		I	
hold		if	
home		immediate	
hope		immediately	
hospital		important	
hospitals		in	
hour		include	
hours		included	
house		includes	
how		including	
however		income	
hundred		increase	

increased		*issue*		
indicate		*issued*		
indicated		*it*		
individual		item		
industrial		items		
industry		its		
inform				
information		*idea*		
informed		*impossible*		
initial		*improve*		
installation		*indeed*		
installed		*influence*		
instance		*instruction*		
instructions		*iron*		
insurance		*itself★*		
interest				
interested				
into		job		
inventory		*just*		
investment				
invoice		*January*		
invoices		*judge*		
involved		*July*		
is		*June*		

91

keep		*less*	
kind		*let*	
kindly		*letter*	
know		*letters*	
		level	
		liability	
king		*life*	
knew		*like*	
knowledge		*line*	
		lines	
		list	
laboratory		listed	
labour		lists	
land		*little*	
large		loading	
larger		loan	
last		local	
late		located	
later		location	
lease		*long*	
least		*longer*	
leave		*look*	
left		looking	
length		*loss*	

lot			make	
low			making	
lower			*man*	
			management	
language			manager	
law			manner	
lead			*many*	
learn			*market*	
light			material	
limit			materials	
live			*matter*	
love			maximum	
			may/May	
			me	
machine			means	
machines			medical	
made			*meet*	
mail			meeting	
mailed			member	
mailing			members	
main			membership	
maintain			men	
maintenance			mentioned	
major			merchandise	

method	....	mass	....
might	....	master	....
mill	....	*meal*	....
mind	....	mean	....
minimum	....	*measure*	....
model	....	meat	....
money	....	memory	....
month	....	mile	....
monthly	....	milk	....
months	....	million	....
more	....	mine★	....
morning	....	minute	....
mortgage	....	miss	....
most	....	Mr	....
motor	....	modern	....
much	....	moment	....
must	....	Monday	....
my	....	mother	....
		move	....
maid★	....	myself	....
manufacture★	....		
March	....		
mark	....	name	....
marry	....	names	....

nature		*news*	
near		*November*	
necessary		*night*	
need		*nor★*	
net			
never			
new		obtain	
next		obtained	
no		of	
No., *number*		off	
normal		offer	
north		office	
not		official	
note		oil	
noted		old	
nothing		on	
notice		once	
now		one	
numbers		only	
nursing		open	
		opening	
		operating	
nation		operation	
neither		operations	

95

opinion		ought	
opportunity		ourselves	
or			
order			
orders		page	
organisation		paid	
original		paper	
other		paragraph	
others		part	
our		particular	
out		particularly	
outlined		parts	
outside		passed	
outstanding		past	
over		patient	
own		patients	
		pay	
object		payable	
observation		payment	
October		payments	
often		pension	
oh/owe*		people	
operate		per	
organise		performance	

perhaps		*possibility*	
period		*possible*	
permit		possibly	
person		*power*	
personal		premises	
personnel		premium	
phone		prepared	
pieces		*present*	
pipe		presently	
place		pressure	
placed		previous	
plan		previously	
plans		*price*	
plant		prices	
please		printing	
pleased		prior	
pleasure		probably	
plus		problem	
p.m.		problems	
point		procedure	
points		procedures	
policy		proceed	
portion		process	
position		produce	

97

production		*purpose*	
product		purposes	
products		put	
profit			
program/ programme		*paint*	
progress		*party*	
project		*pass*	
promotion		*peace/piece*	
prompt		*pence*	
proper		*perfect*	
properly		*picture*	
property		*plain/plane*★	
proposal		*play*★	
proposed		*political*★	
protection		*poor*	
provide		*pound*, lb	
provided		*principal/principle*	
providing		*probable*	
province		*pull*	
provincial			
public			
purchase		*quality*	
purchased		quantities	
purchasing		quantity	

98

question		receiving	
questions		*recent*	
quite		recently	
quotation		recommend	
quote		*record*	
quoted		records	
		red	
quarter		reduce	
quick		refer	
		reference	
		referred	
rate		*regard*	
rates		regarding	
rather		regards	
re		registered	
ready		registration	
realise		*regret*	
reason		*regular*	
reasonable		regulations	
reasons		remain	
recall		rental	
receipt		repairs	
receive		replacement	
received		reply	

99

report		room	
reported		run	
reports			
representative		radio	
request		rail ★	
requested		reach	
requesting		read	
require		real ★	
required		really	
requirements		relate	
research		remember	
reserve		represent	
respect		rest/wrest	
responsibility		river	
responsible		round	
result		rule	
results			
retail			
return		said	
returned		sale	
returning		sales	
review		same	
right		sample	
road		samples	

satisfactory		shall	
savings		share	
say		shareholders	
schedule		shares	
school		she	
season		sheet	
second		sheets	
section		ship	
see		shipment	
seem		shipments	
seems		shipped	
sell		shipping	
selling		short	
send		should	
sending		show	
sent		showing	
separate		shown	
serve		shows	
service		side	
services		sign	
set		signed	
sets		similar	
settlement		since	
several		single	

101

site		stocks	
situation		storage	
six		*store*	
size		stores	
small		*street*	
so		students	
sold		study	
some		*subject*	
something		submit	
soon		submitted	
sorry		successful	
space		*such*	
special		sufficient	
specific		*suggest*	
specifications		suggested	
staff		suggestion	
standard		suggestions	
start		suitable	
stated		supplied	
statement		*supply*	
statements		support	
steel		*sure*	
still		survey	
stock		*system*	

102

safe		station	
sail		steal	
Saturday		step	
save		stone	
scene/seen		stop	
science★		story	
sea		straight	
self		strange	
sense★		strong	
September		success	
serious		sum	
sew/sow★		summer	
simple		Sunday	
sir		surprise	
sit		sweet	
sometimes			
sort			
sound		take	
south		taken	
speak		taking	
spend		tax	
spent		taxes	
stand		telephone	
state		tell	

ten		through	
term		throughout	
terms		thus	
test		*time*	
tests		times	
than		*to*	
thank		today	
thanking		*together*	
thanks		tons	
that		*too*	
the		top	
their		total	
them		*touch*	
then		training	
there		transfer	
therefore		trip	
these		*trouble*	
they		truck	
think		*trust*	
third		trusting	
this		*two*	
those		type	
thought			
three		*table*	

104

talk		understand	
teach		understanding	
television		unfortunately	
themselves		unit	
thing		units	
though		unless	
thousand		*until*	
Thursday		*up*	
till★		*upon*	
told		*us*	
tomorrow		*use*	
toward/trade		*used*	
town		*using*	
train		*usual*	
tried			
true			
truth		*value*	
try		various	
Tuesday		vehicle	
turn		*very*	
		vessel	
		via	
unable		*view*	
under		visit	

volume		why	
		will	
voice		winter	
		wish	
		wishes	
want		with	
warehouse		within	
was		without	
water		work	
way		working	
we		would	
week		write	
weeks		writer	
weight		writing	
welcome		written	
well			
were		waist	
what		walk	
when		war	
where		warm	
whether		waste	
which		watch	
while		weak	
who		Wednesday	

weigh		*word*	
went		*world*	
west		*worth*	
whatever		*wrong*	
whenever			
white			
whole		*year*	
whom		*years*	
whose		*yesterday*	
wide		*yet*	
window		*you*	
wire★		*your*	
wise		*yourself*	
woman			
women		*yard*	
wonderful		*yes*	
wonderfully		*young*	

APPENDIX: *Useful phrases*

UNIT 1

Passage 1

in respect of the

you have

if this is

please let us have

of this letter

of course

we do not

Yours faithfully

Passage 2

it is sometimes

of these
  arrangements
application form

Passage 3

in our notice

electricity charges

new charges

most likely

we hope you will

it is not possible

but we may be
  able to

Passage 4

copy of

number of

to have been

UNIT 2

Passage 2

last month's

as soon as possible

before the end

of this month

interest charges

Yours sincerely

Passage 3

easier than

will be able to

your enquiries

if it is convenient

Passage 4		Passage 3	
we have been		it is suggested	
would not have been		particular requirements	
who have			
Annual General Meeting		**Passage 4**	
you will be required		specialist company	
		therefore arranged	
Passage 5		take the form of	
if it is		who have been	

UNIT 3

Passage 1

our own	
better than	
in reply to your request	
quantity of	
if you require	
supply of	

Passage 2

in the first instance	
for your consideration	
your requirements	
next week	

UNIT 4

Passage 1

also require	
I would	
of our attention	
at all times	

Passage 2

| and would like | |

Passage 3

business lunch	
to this arrangement	

Passage 4

always been

particular attention

in business

as a result

will you please

will be required

UNIT 5

Passage 1

Oil Company

in accordance with

be able to charge

Law Association's

Passage 2

last month

at the moment

Passage 3

copy of

as soon as
  we have

Passage 4

next door

six months

on this matter

UNIT 6

Passage 1

600

700 words

black and white

2,000 words

Passage 2

name and address

no later than

Passage 3

must be

Passage 5

on this subject

UNIT 7

Passage 1

receipt of

next month

we must have

Passage 2

annual charge

in our own

Passage 3

to begin

Passage 4

will be required

and we will
  arrange
your consideration

point of view

UNIT 8

Passage 1

as soon as it is

Passage 2

will have their

at all times

Passage 3

small charge

each of the

Passage 4

Annual Business

free of charge

UNIT 9

Passage 1

report forms

Passage 2

in charge of

as quickly as
  possible

Passage 3

let us have

Passage 4

which we would

it seems to me

UNIT 10

Passage 1

to be considered

Accounts
  Department
application form

Passage 2

draw your attention

age of

will you please let me know the

Passage 3

for some time

and that you will not be

at all

to be made

Passage 4

to appear

Officer's Department

must be able to

please arrange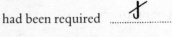

UNIT 11

Passage 1

had been required

Passage 2

for the attention

on your part

and we would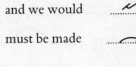

must be made

Passage 3

first class

copy of the

Passage 4

I would

in other parts

medical requirements

your own arrangements

and I will arrange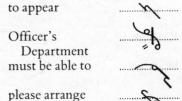

UNIT 12

Passage 1

at once

is to be

to be used

Passage 2

Personnel Department

another department

in accordance with the

from the Department

her own

from time to
time
seems to be

if it is possible

Passage 3

specialist
attention
of one of our own

for the Company

Passage 4

there appears

up-to-date

age of the

UNIT 13

Passage 1

they would like

next month

Passage 2

Out Patients'
Department

Passage 3

use of computers

various
departments
in respect of

I hope that this

Passage 4

you will not

your own

any one time

UNIT 14

Passage 1

Car Company

above Company

no longer

must be sent

for the attention

Passage 2

telephone
conversation
in respect of
the charges
early reply

Passage 3

back of the

new form

113

Passage 4

advantage of the

as soon as it

UNIT 15

Passage 1

dresses required

premium required

Passage 2

past experience

Passage 3

Proposal Form

Passage 4

Report Form

of this form

their enquiries

UNIT 16

Passage 1

every attention

Passage 2

we hope you
will not

in reply to your
enquiry
customers'
requirements

Passage 3

instead of

Passage 4

they will only be

in the case of

UNIT 17

Passage 1

it is only

shortage of

degree of

at the moment

will you please
consider
on the committee

Passage 2

three months

has been arranged

that this would
have
side of the
common

Passage 3

to become

member of

neighbour of the

UNIT 18

Passage 1

in fact

once again

if you are not

Passage 2

50 per cent

100 per cent

finance charges

Passage 3

twelve months

Passage 4

business
    relationship
second charge

rate of interest

Passage 5

Staff Association

exchange of

UNIT 19

Passage 1

2½ per cent

Passage 2

from your Company

Passage 3

claim form

one of our
    Company's
immediate
    arrangements
rental company

Passage 4

and compliments

standard forms

on us

UNIT 20

Passage 1

out of date

on the subject

Passage 3

in business

at one time

personal		if there is	
attention			
to take part		anything else	

Passage 4

no longer